Milton Regis Remembered

A story of a town and its people

Milton Regis Remembered

A story of a town and its people

Members of
The Freedom Centre

FREEDOM CENTRE PUBLISHING
SHEERNESS KENT

Other publications:
Blue Town Remembered   1992 (out of print)
Around and About the Isle of Sheppey   1995 ISBN 0 9520220 1 X

Published by
Freedom Centre Publishing
St Georges Avenue, Sheerness,
Kent ME12 1QT
Tel: 01795 666233
Fax: 01795 666239

Freedom Centre 1999

ISBN 0 9520220 2 8

Cover illustrations
Front: A view of Milton High Street circa 1900

Courtesy Margaret & Bill Lee and Alan Cordell
Back: A busy scene at Milton Creek in the early part of the 1900s

All rights reserved. No part of this publication may be reproduced, transmitted or stored in any means, electronic or mechanical, including photocopying, recording, or any information storage and retrieval system, without prior written permission of the publisher.

Printed in Great Britain by
Island Printers,
Granville Place, Granville Road,
Sheerness, Kent, ME12 1QR
Tel/Fax: 01795 662680

ACKNOWLEDGEMENTS

This book is a project of the social history class of the Freedom Centre (Working with people with physical disabilities aged 16-64). Registered Charity Number: 1007683.

It was researched, written and compiled by:
Beryl Kingsnorth
Dennis J Smith

Cover design by Dennis J. Smith

Freedom Centre Publishing would like to thank everyone who helped with this book.

Dr Robert Baxter (*Court Hall Museum*)
Barbara Cullen
Mrs Chris Kite (*Manager Freedom Centre*)
Mr Pearson (*Headmaster, Milton Court Primary School*)
Fred Sands
Wendy Shepherd
Staff of Reference Section (*Sittingbourne Library*)
The Members of Milton Regis Bowls Club including:
President: Ken Rees
Chairman: Dave Nichols
Eddie and Jill Long

Many thanks to Court Hall Museum, Margaret and Bill Lee and Alan Cordell (Sittingbourne and District in Pictures) Mr and Mrs Clark, Milton Tea Rooms and Peter Mantle for the loan of their precious photographs. Special Thanks to Jeff Wilson.

The "Royal and Ancient" Borough of Milton Regis
Court Hall Museum
The Mid 15th century timbered building once used as a Courthouse, School and Town Gaol.

Milton Regis retains a character of its own.
The Museum has a fine display of photographs and documents.

Well worth a visit

Open Saturdays 2-5pm
April to September.

CONTENTS

INTRODUCTION

BOOK I - MIDDLETUN TO MILTON
1. THE BEGINNING - *12*
2. THE CHURCH - *13*
3. THE BOWLS CLUB - *16*
4. THE CREEK - *23*
5. THE TOWN - *24*
6. COURT HALL - *25*
7. THE PEOPLE - *27*
8. LOCAL INDUSTRIES - *28*
9. PUBLIC HOUSES - *The Three Hats - 31*
10. THE TOWN - *32*
11. THE BRICKFIELDS - *36*
12. CEMENT - *40*
13. THE PAPER MILL - *41*
14. NON-CONFORMIST CHURCHES - *The Congregational - 45*
15. THE WORKHOUSE - *49*
16. SCHOOLS - *54*

BOOK II MILTON IN THE 19th CENTURY
1. THE TOWN - *64*
2. LOCAL INDUSTRIES - *67*
3. TRANSPORT - *Barges - Railways - 69*
4. THE FIRE BRIGADE - *71*
5. SOCIAL LIFE - *72*
6. THE COFFEE TAVERN - *74*
7. THE PERIWINKLE - *75*
8. ST PAUL'S CHURCH - *75*
9. THE TOWN - *76*

BOOK III MILTON REGIS IN THE 20th CENTURY
1 THE FIRST DECADE - *80*
2 THE FIRST WORLD WAR - *82*
3 THE 1920s AND 30s - *87*
4 THE SECOND WORLD WAR - *92*
5 THE 1950s AND 60s - *100*
6 MEMORIES OF GROWING UP - *108*
7 MEMORIES OF WORK AND PASTIMES - *130*
8 MEMORIES OF PUB LIFE - *137*
9 PRESENT AND FUTURE - *144*

PUBLIC HOUSES IN 1908 - *150*
GLOSSARY - *151*

THE HEART OF MILTON
IN 1900

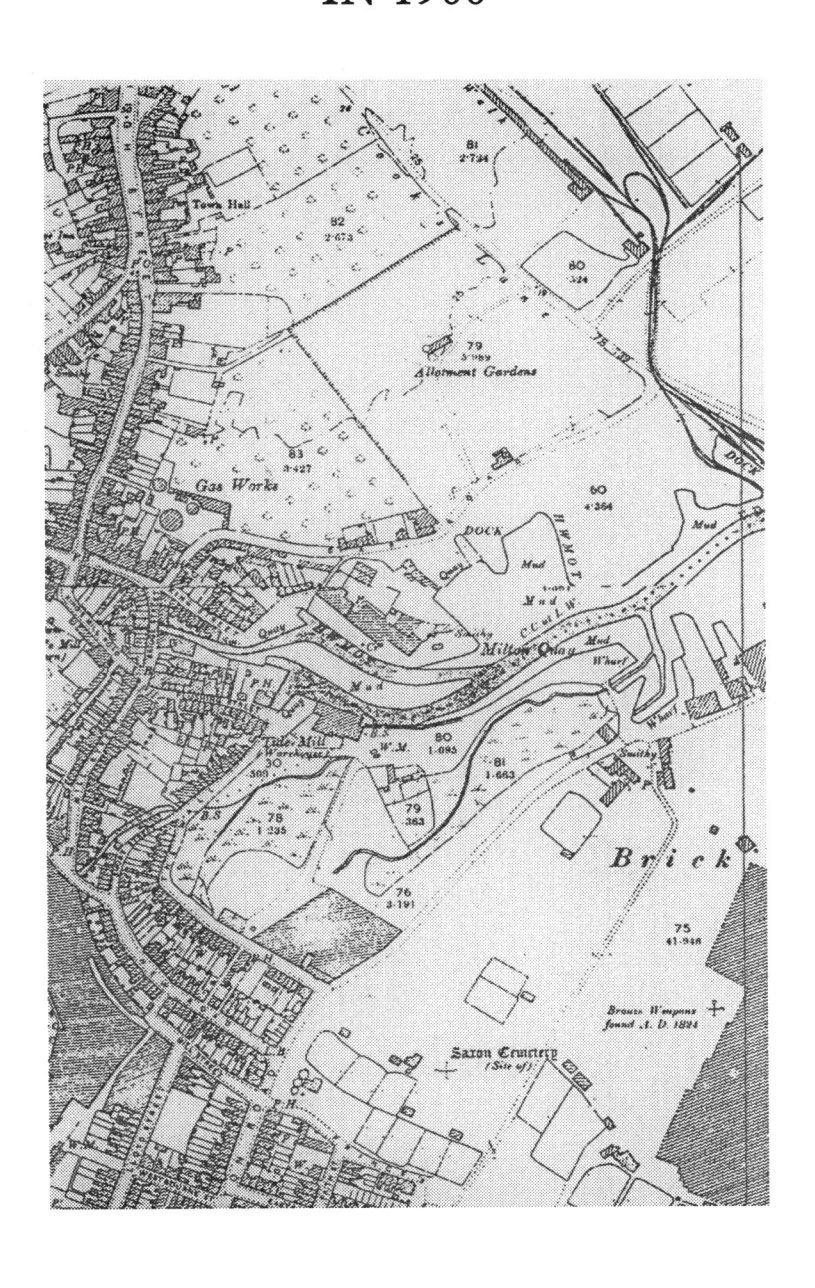

INTRODUCTION

People travelling from the Isle of Sheppey probably regard Milton Regis as a small town that they have to pass in order to reach Sittingbourne or the A2 to Canterbury and Dover. Milton Regis is so much more than that! It was originally called the King's Town of Middletun because of its position in the middle of the old English Kingdom of Kent and throughout many centuries it was one of the crown's possessions. Situated 40 miles south east of London, Middletun came into being during the seventh century. It was the administrative centre for the Milton Hundred and through the years has seen many changes. It started life as a fishing village, then in turn: a flourishing port, a mill town, home for the manufacturing of bricks and cement and eventually, an industrial town. All this was there as well as enough fertile ground for farms and orchards. The town, during the early years was referred to as Middletun, Middletune, Middleton, Middletone, the King's Royal Milton and then Milton next Sittingbourne before finally becoming Milton Regis; but although throughout the years the name and the town itself have changed several times the people have always been hardworking, loyal, cheerful and friendly.

Book One

Middletun to Milton

1. THE BEGINNING

The town of Middletun, in those early days, stretched from the higher London Road (Watling Street) northwards to the waters of the Swale. In the small hamlet in the south, called Chalkwell because of the soil, there were several springs which fed a stream, called the Periwinkle, which in turn filled a reservoir. This was eventually used to work two mills before forming part of the creek. There it was joined by the larger stream which ran from a pond at Bredgar, called Hart's Delight, a watering hole for animals and which is now a road called Heart's Delight, down through what later became Ufton Lane and Cockleshell Walk.

A third stream, known as the Bourne, entered the creek from the east at Crown Quay. This creek, of course, is the reason for the town's existence because the waters of the creek led to the Swale, meeting the Thames at the mouth of the River Medway. From the Swale the water flowed to Reculver where it joined the River Wantsume which originally separated the Isle of Thanet from the mainland. From there it flowed to Richborough and so into the English Channel. The position of the town made it a very important place.

Most of the Kingdom of Kent was thickly wooded and as Middletune was one of the few areas that was clear it was ideal for the settlements of people from the earliest times. It was popular as far back as the Iron and Bronze Ages and relics of those times have been found nearby. There is also a great deal of evidence to show that the Romans had settlements here. For example, in the late 19th Century six lead coffins belonging to that era were found at Bexhill, one of which was presented to Maidstone museum.

The period of time from the Romans leaving until the Norman Conquest was called the Dark Ages because very little was known about life in England. The Milton area was home to Anglo Saxons and marauding Danes and the Kingdom of Kent saw many upheavals.

In the year 892 the Viking, Hasten, accompanied by 80 ships, invaded the town, and legend has it that he built the fortress known as Castle Rough (although subsequent findings throw some doubt on this). The Vikings were finally expelled by King Alfred who had his own fortress, Bayford Castle, built on the other side of the creek in 983.

In 1052 Earl Godwin quarrelled with Edward the Confessor and the King's Royal Town of Milton, being a royal manor, was considered a fair target and destroyed along with most of the church. The creek was tidal and the town subject to much flooding and so it was decided to build the new town at the head of the creek, although the original site was kept for the new church. Legend has it that the local people wanted to build the church nearer the new town but after the foundations had been laid in their new position they were removed during the night and taken back to the site of the old church. After this happened a second time they thought perhaps it was the work of God and the church was duly built on the original site leaving it standing out in the marshes, half a mile from everywhere.

2. THE CHURCH

The church is one of the oldest in Kent. Built in the seventh century, the original one was much smaller consisting only of a Nave and a Sanctuary. A connection to the Isle of Sheppey was made when, in the year 680, Queen Sexburga of Kent, the founder of Minster Abbey, died in the doorway. The new church was built on the site of the old one, keeping the north wall with its Saxon and Roman materials. The rest of the building was built of flint and ragstone.

In the eleventh century the Normans built the Chancel and the South Transept. The remains of the latter form part of the south wall and it is now the same height as the Chancel. The yearly amounts paid to Canterbury at this time included: 30 pounds of honey, 2 multones, 8 lambs, 60 loaves, 12d for consecrated oil and 600d. This was far more than any other church and probably points to the importance of the town.

Holy Trinity Church pictured in 1908 when there was a lake near by.

The Sacristy was built in the thirteenth century but the doorway which connects it to the Chancel is early English and therefore probably original. In the fourteenth century the church was enlarged with the addition of a porch, the south aisle and the tower; the latter is one of the largest in the country. It is 27 feet square inside with walls 94 feet high and 4 feet thick. During the next century a chapel was built on for the use of one of the leading families of the time, the de Northwodes. A member of this family married into the Norton family who lived near Faversham. Sir John Norton was the Sheriff of Kent in 1514 and is buried in the chapel in Milton Church.

The church register of baptisms and burials date from 1538 and the register of marriages from 1622. By 1681 the church tower boasted of 5 bells and the church had 800 sittings, nearly all free. Up until the late 19th century the parish church had box pews which separated the congregation according to their status because everyone went to church, rich and poor alike. Anyone who fell asleep during the sermon could expect to be rudely woken by a beadle who walked round carrying a wand of office for this purpose.

There being no organ in those days the choir sang accompanied by a clarinet, oboe and viola. Up until the middle of the nineteenth century the curfew bell was still being rung, from Michaelmas to Lady Day at 4am and 8pm.

Because the church was so far away from the main part of the town it was decided in 1859 to build a Chapel of Ease and so the numbers of people attending the Holy Trinity depleted. The church fell into disrepair but the local people did not like the idea of it being pulled down. During the late nineteenth century Queen Victoria ordered many churches in the country to be restored and the one at Milton was no exception. Many repairs were made and the Tower Screen and the box pews were removed. New pews were installed and tiles laid and in the early 20th century more work was done including new stained glass in the east window and a communion rail. In 1970 a new Tower Screen was built.

A very memorable church service was held in 1949. It was broadcast on the BBC World Service and there was a large congregation present to witness the event. The choirmaster was Arthur Beach and all the choirboys were happy to take part because they used to receive 5 shillings every three months and extra money for other occasions.

The church tower added in the 14th century. One of the tallest in the country.

In 1982 the church faced another crisis when money was badly needed to do repairs to the building. These included replacing part of the roof due to the lead being stolen. The Vicar, the Reverend William Drury, was reported as saying that when it rained there were waterfalls inside, causing untold damage. £60,000 was needed to pay for the repairs and at one point it looked as though the church was in danger of losing its resident vicar, which meant that eventually it would have to close. An appeal made locally in November raised the level of the donations by 18% in that month and by 30% during the first few months of the following year. The church architects stated that with support from the Historic Buildings Council and other grants the most urgent repairs could be done at once but it would take up to ten years to do all that needed doing.

This Holy Trinity Church at Milton Regis has stood for nine hundred years, surviving acts of vandalism, erosion, arson and neglect.

3. THE BOWLS CLUB

Some five hundred years after the church was rebuilt and a few hundred yards down the road came Milton Regis Bowling Club which is thought to be the oldest one in England, dating

Four yew trees at the Bowls Club, Five hundred years old.

from 1540, although there are those who would question this. There can be no doubt, however, that the area known as The Butts, where the green is situated, was certainly in existence before this date. It was primarily used for archery practice as the youths of the land were made to practise their skills in order to be ready for any wars that might occur, there being no regular army. The yew trees which still stand there are at least five hundred years old and the wood from yew trees was used to make the longbows.

It is known that well before this date the game of bowls was forbidden by several monarchs as it was thought the game interfered with archery practice. Because of this there are few records of bowling clubs before the year 1640 and as the fine for being convicted of bowling was 6s 8d the only likely source of records would be the court ones. The name of Sir Francis Drake has been linked with Milton, as his father was the Vicar of Upchurch. The link is strengthened by the fact that Drake was known to become interested in sailing and the sea at an early age and of course in the sixteenth century Milton was a very busy port.

Up until 1960 the land on which the Bowling Club stood belonged to the Church and the first understandable written reference to the green can be found in the Church Warden Accounts of Holy Trinity Church, Milton, dated after 1640. Anything before this was written in Latin or Middle English.

The first article written in a local newspaper about Milton Bowling Club appeared in 1862 when it was reported that a fireworks display was held on the bowling green and later in the same year the children from Milton National School had their annual treat on the green. Not long after this reports of matches appeared in the newspaper and, interestingly, these matches were between members not against other clubs.

The club also took part in the traditions of the town and on St James' day in 1867 the annual fair was held at Milton Butts. Only a few people attended this event and there were not many attractions. The end of the day found those attending at the 'Three Hats' public house at the top of Milton Hill. It was reported that in 1892 a number of ladies played bowls at the yearly gathering and 120 people enjoyed a splendid tea. During the evening, with the place lit by hundreds of fairy lights, dancing took place and the first dance was led by Mr Goodhew, aged 86 and Aunt Baker, aged 90. The dances included the lancers and quadrilles.

By 1920 Association Bowls had been in existence for some time and Milton Regis had been considering the change very seriously. An Extraordinary General Meeting was held in November 1924 at which the membership voted to have an Association Green next to the Crown Green. The 1925 Annual General Meeting of Milton Bowling Club was held in March, at the Town Hall, with the Chairman of the Council presiding. Great interest was being shown in the game since the creation of the Association Green because members could now play under both sets of rules on the adjacent greens. A lot of work had been carried out during the previous year in repairs and renovations. A new summerhouse had been built and a large section of turf laid. Membership had increased from 86 to 107. Thanks were given to Messrs Edward Lloyd Limited for providing the turf from their land at Kemsley. On Wednesday June 10th 1925 the opening ceremony of the new Association Green was performed by Mr R B Miller.

In 1934 the Rev J N Wells, Vicar of Milton Regis, who was also the club president, dared to suggest that women be allowed as playing members. He pointed out that the Sittingbourne Club already had women members and he felt that women had earned the right to join by all the work that they had done for the club. It was also suggested that by allowing women to join, the membership would be increased which in turn would help to pay off the club's debts. It was decided at the meeting to refer the matter to the committee who duly agreed and at last a ladies' section was started. It was the custom of the club not to take minutes of their Annual General Meetings, instead to rely on the report written in the East Kent Gazette. The year following the start of the ladies' section it was discovered that no one had brought a copy and so no minutes could be read.

Bowls Club members at prize giving 1948. Among those pictured are: Dick Taylor, Arthur Palmer, Albert Cattermole, Bill Burgess, Majorie and Cyril Carpenter, E H Coupland, Burt Jordan, Harry Smith, Captain, Malcolm and Rose Giles, Ted Inge, Harold and Vera Ford. E Bugge, Alf Curtis and Burt Taylor, Chairman.

For a number of years only friendly games could be played on the Association Green as it was too small for competitions but this changed in 1939 when the site of the old crown green was used to form part of a bigger green, and this is still in use today. This was a great turning point in the history of the club as in the true spirit of Miltonians the members raised enough money to pay for the conversion and also for the building of a new locker room and an extension to the pavilion. Therefore the club could celebrate the opening in the knowledge that no debts had been incurred.

Of course the coming of World War II put an end to much of the club's activities as many members were involved in essential work but, nevertheless, 1940 saw the formation of the Sittingbourne and Milton Regis Bowling Club league. Milton Regis, Lloyds, Kemsley and Sittingbourne made up the league and the entry fee was 10 shillings.

For some years after the war membership was low even though, in 1946, £40.17s.2d was spent on extending the green so that members could play both ways. Improvements continued to be made and in 1954 electricity was installed at a cost of £21.15s.6d. About this time, too, the ladies' section paid for the gas fire heating. This cost £16.18s.7d.

In 1958 the ladies section requested permission to play on the men's green as the condition of the one the ladies played on was deteriorating rapidly. This was agreed with certain conditions. One of these was that the ladies pay the full annual subscription plus the greenage fees and the other was that when the men were playing the ladies would be confined to one rink and would only be allowed to play in the afternoons. This rule was changed the following year and the ladies were not allowed to play at all when the men were playing a match.

The closure of the Sittingbourne Bowls club in 1959, due to redevelopment, caused two things to happen at Milton. One was that some of the members transferred to Milton thus increasing the membership considerably and the other was the very generous offers from Mr E Bugge and Mr B Cattermole to pay for the purchase of the ground from the church which gave the club security of tenure. A wish was expressed by one of the donors that there should still be no play on a Sunday even though the church no longer owned the ground. This was agreed. The two men also bought a strip of land on the eastern side of the green a year later when it was put on the market.

The members of the club became heavily involved in this new project, not only by raising funds to pay for the work that needed to be done but by also doing some of the work themselves; for example: by clearing out privet hedges. The chairman of the day, Mr H Butcher, was full of praise for the way everyone worked together and on the 11th May 1966 the new extension to the green was officially opened by Cllr Easton of Sittingbourne & Milton Urban District Council. The cost was £856.

By 1969 a new pavilion had been built and it was decided to

name it after the chairman in recognition of all his hard work and so it was called 'The Hedley Butcher Pavilion'. At this time the local council allocated a three year grant towards the running of the club. During the next few years much time and effort was put in by the members to help the club. An extension was added to the pavilion and the old changing room was demolished with a new one built in its place. Although the council and the Sports Council gave the club grants and loans none of this would have happened without the members all working and pulling together.

Grand opening of new facilities at Bowls Club. 1998

During the late 1980s some notable events took place at the club. Cllr Peter Morgan was the Mayor of Swale in 1987 and he asked the club if they would organise something to celebrate the 400th anniversary of the defeat of the Spanish Armada in 1588. The members were fired with enthusiasm for this idea and on the 4th of July 1988 an Elizabethan Bowls match was staged for which there was newspaper, radio and television coverage. Taking part were the children from the Holy Trinity School,

Upchurch and from Middletune School, Milton Regis. A great carnival atmosphere was added by the staging of Elizabethan games, dancing and music by the children from the Butts Infants School. The whole thing was organised by Mr Don Kent, the club secretary.

The success of the Armada Day was enhanced when, in that same year, Dave Nichols, the club captain, Ken Rees, Dave Hoddinott and Alan Hill all won their county badges. Alan Milan added to the success by reaching the county finals in the Unbadged Singles and in the following year he, along with Ron Roullier and Bill Campbell reached the County Finals thereby adding another badge to the club's collection.

In 1989 Marion Luckhurst made a grand birthday cake which featured a Wyvern in the club's colours for the occasion of the 50th anniversary of the Ladies Section. This celebration took place on July 6th during an anniversary match with a number of local clubs.

During the 1990s the members of Milton Regis bowling club have been playing against patients from the Stoke Mandeville hospital, on their own green and at the hospital on alternate years. This has proved to be very successful with everyone enjoying the events enormously. The members have also undertaken a great deal of fundraising with the proceeds going to a different charity each year. There are social members as well as playing members and the methods used to raise money are quite unconventional. For example someone may be fined one day for doing something, such as wearing a tie, and the next time they go to the club they will be fined for not doing the same thing.

Money from the Sports Division of the National Lottery enabled the club in 1998 to build new changing rooms and this was opened by the Member of Parliament for Sittingbourne and Sheppey, Derek Wyatt at a special ceremony. The grounds and buildings are now all completely accessible to people in wheelchairs.

Photograph taken in 1998 of ground which is wheelchair friendly.

4. THE CREEK

At the heart of Milton and supplying its life's blood was the creek. For many centuries it allowed Milton to be a thriving centre for all water transport with sailing barges carrying goods such as meat, wool, grain, fruit, vegetables and hops to London and returning with sugar, wine and coal and the few other necessities of life not available locally. A number of barges were too big to enter the creek and smaller vessels such as smacks and lighters were used to ferry the goods between the quays and the barges and hoys were used to carry goods and passengers along the coast. Many of the inhabitants earned their living on the water either working on the barges or by fishing, including dredging for oysters.

One of the quays was Fluddmill which was a tide mill at the creek's head. In the sixteenth century it was worked by means of sluices which controlled the flow of water into a five acre holding pond. A story is told of how boys in later years used to use their mothers' forks tied to sticks to try and catch flounders by the sluices.

5. THE TOWN

In the Domesday Book, 1086, Milton is listed as Terra Regis (land of the King). William the Conqueror had discovered that the Manor of Milton was very rich and took it for his own. The manor at the time of the Domesday Survey was estimated at 10,000 acres and worth about £200. It stated that there were 309 villeins and 24 bordarers. Villeins being peasants who gave service to the Lord of the Manor and a bordarer being a cottager with a little land of his own. The Manor contained 6 mills, 18 acres of pasture, 24 saltpans and 32 fisheries. He gave the tenancy to the Norman barons, the one at this time being Hogo de Port.

By this time the town had been rebuilt at the head of the creek, on a hill, as the surrounding area was very marshy and subject to much flooding. Milton itself was the head of the

Old painting of market, situated in the middle of the High Street, in front of Middletune House.

'Hundred of Milton', an administrative centre for the whole area, stretching from the Isle of Sheppey and the Swale in the north to Bredgar and Milstead in the south and from Rainham in the west to Bapchild and Tonge in the east.

The right to hold a market in the town was granted by Isabella, wife of King Edward II in 1319 and lasted until 1878. The people were also allowed to hold a three day fair once a year, starting on July 24th. The town's market cross and clock house stood in the middle of the High Street, in an area known as The Shambles, until 1803. The bell that was used for the market was also the means of summoning people to church, funerals and parish meetings.

During the reign of Queen Elizabeth I it was noted that Milton had 130 houses and 4 quays, namely: Fluddmill, Whitlock's, Reynold's, and Hammond's, compared with Sittingbourne which consisted only of 88 houses and 2 quays. According to the survey undertaken by the historian, Hasted, by 1778 Milton had grown into a town containing 230 houses with 1200 inhabitants. There were also 5 mills, 5 quays and 32 fisheries.

6. COURT HALL

1450 saw the building of Court Hall in the heart of the town. This was the centre for all judicial and administrative affairs. Court sessions were held here and all people found guilty were incarcerated in the prison that formed part of the building. The gratings of the cells through which the prisoners used to be fed by their families can still be seen today. The stocks and a pillory were built nearby and it can be assumed that there was also a gallows. During the reign of Charles I the building was used as a school and later in the seventeenth century marriage ceremonies were performed there.

One event that took place in Court Hall annually was the choosing of the local Portreeve. This was a very important position because the person chosen controlled the port and the market and supervised the weights and measures and was entitled to a percentage of the dues on imported coal. By 1851 the position of Portreeve was not so lucrative as an Act of Parliament took two thirds of the income from the Portreeve to pay for the paving of the streets. The last Portreeve was Sydney Nicholls in the 1920s and with the end of the Manorial system, making Court Hall superfluous, he bought it at a cost of £75. He died in 1947 and the building was purchased by Councillor Thomas Buggs. In 1956 the Council wanted to demolish it but thanks to the efforts of Councillor Buggs and the local press it was saved and restored. Court Hall has been a museum since 1972, run by the Sittingbourne Archaeology group for Swale Borough Council.

Court Hall built in 1450, photographed in 1999.

MEMORIES OF PETER MANTLE

My grandfather was the last person to be locked up in Court Hall. He was found to be drunk and disorderly and he was put in the dungeon. The reason this happened was because he had a habit of going into the Conservative Club with a Labour rosette on and shouting, 'You've 'ad it, next time. You're going to be well beaten.'

It was better for the club to let him stay and get drunk than to throw him out. And that's how he came to be locked up in Court Hall.

7. THE PEOPLE OF MILTON

As the town was built in the middle of farmland and marshland and was miles from any other place the people were, no doubt, a very close knit community and well able to cope with life. Indeed, if it had not been for the vessels entering the creek from foreign ports they might never have known of events going on anywhere else. There was no way they could travel over land, only the few, richer people had carriages or carts drawn by horses. There were no newspapers or post and almost everything they needed was there, around them.

During times of unrest in the country, however, the people were always ready and willing to take part in national affairs when called upon to do so. This was especially true when their way of life was affected, as with the Poll Tax, which in the late 14th century was introduced to raise money to pay for a war against France. Wat Tyler's followers in the rebellion against this tax included many from the Milton area.

In May 1450 there was another rebellion which involved many local men. This was not only against the high taxes which people had to pay but also against the very harsh labour laws which were prevalent at this time. The men rose up and followed the leader of the rebellion, John Cade. They came from all parts of the county, assembled at Maidstone and by the time they were ready to march they numbered 20,000. When they reached London Bridge the forces of the King were waiting for them and battle was joined and the rebellion put down. All of Cade's followers were granted a pardon provided that they went home. Cade was also pardoned by the King but he lost it a short while later for leaving the area and going to Rochester Castle.

There were other riots over the years the most notable one being against the Corn Laws in the early eighteenth century.

Compared to much of the country, however, the Milton Hundred was quite wealthy and so there were not so many uprisings as elsewhere.

8. LOCAL INDUSTRIES

Throughout the years until the middle of the nineteenth century life did not change for the people of Milton; they earned their living by working on or by the creek and also on the farms of the surrounding Milton Hundred. These two seemingly different ways of life were very much dependent on each other with produce from the farms providing cargo for the barges to carry to London and other large towns.

Some of the meat produced on the farms was sold in Milton market, which made more jobs for local people. Because the Hundred covered a large area and therefore consisted of various types of soil, cattle and sheep were farmed as well as a wealth of corn, vegetables, fruit, and hops.

On market days the town came alive with the hustle and bustle of the people working, with sounds and smells filling the air and the red sails of the barges on the water providing a colourful backdrop to the scene. Much trading was done there, and although fruit, vegetables, fish and oysters were sold, meat was the principal commodity on offer.

Meat, of course, was not the only product obtained from the farm animals; tallow was produced from the melted down fat which was used to make candles; wool, of course, came from the sheep and the hides of the cattle were made into leather. One of the earliest businesses in Middleton was the tannery, which was situated at Chalkwell. This was an ideal location for it as it needed to be well away from the town centre because of the smell but close to water that was provided by the Periwinkle stream. The tannery was known to exist before the year 1500. The tanning process was a lengthy business with the skins having to be soaked in various solutions before being dried.

The land at Chalkwell was called 'Taynter Land' and when

the skins were ready they were stretched out on the ground and held down by tenter hooks to keep them taut. Local weavers also used this means of stretching the cloth that they made. The tanning industry gave rise to others that used the leather such as shoemakers, clickers and glovers. Saddle makers also did a roaring trade making things from leather, not only saddles, but also goods such as belts, holsters, purses, and all kinds of bags.

Fishing was a major industry and dredging for oysters had provided a very lucrative way of earning a living for many centuries. In Roman times the shells were crushed and used for medicinal uses. The quality of the oysters found locally was renowned throughout Europe, and they were known as Milton Natives.

Courtesy of Margaret and Bill Lee and Alan Cordell

Kingsmill, Church Street, in an area now developed

There was a wheelwrights and a forge, which was known as Dobbie's Forge and was near the top of Milton Hill, and, of course, there were the mills: the Fluddmill, later known as the Tide Mill, at the head of the creek, the Mede, Kings and Periwinkle Mills at Chalkwell and the Meads near Vicarage

Road. These were all water mills and there was also a windmill near the Meads. These ground the corn which grew in the surrounding area although the Periwinkle also made pearl barley for a while.

At the northern end of the High Street at Spratt's Hill (now known as Sprotshill) there was once a very unusual business. During the reign of Henry VIII the autumnal crocus from which saffron is derived was grown here. Although expensive, saffron was very popular at this time as a flavouring and colouring. The people liked to flavour their food, drink and confectionery with saffron even though it cost from 9d to 1s.2d an ounce. By 1574 records show that the crocuses had been replaced by a cherry orchard. Later, the land was built on with nothing left to show that there was once such exotic foodstuffs grown there.

Sprottshill, once the site of a saffron garden.

Another local industry was brewing; this was done mostly in huts in the gardens of the local inns although people other than innkeepers used their gardens for the brewing of ale.

9. PUBLIC HOUSES

Public houses have always been one of the main places of entertainment in Milton and the 'Three Hats' in the High Street is one that has survived for more than four hundred years. This public house was built in the reign of King Henry VII in the year 1503 and remained unchanged until the reign of George III in the 18th century. It was built as a dwelling house by Thomas Elliott who wanted to use it as a lodging house but in 1512 he sold it. It wasn't until 1539 that it became licensed and the first landlord was one Silas Hazeldene, although in those days he was known simply as an ale keeper and the pub was known as an ale house. After he died his widow sold the premises but it was not licensed to sell ale again until it was purchased by Thomas Snoad, a marine chandler, in 1612. When he died, in 1646, he bequeathed the property to his son, Michael, and the records show that this included a brewhouse.

In 1660 Michael Snoad was granted a licence to sell wines and it was at this time that the name 'The Three Hats' was given to the property. The name derived from three cavaliers who dined there at the time of the restoration of the throne to King Charles II and the original pub sign was of three cavalier hats.

Three Hats, one of the oldest public houses in Milton Regis

During the years that followed the pub changed hands many

times and in 1678 it was bought by a surgeon and apothecary, Thomas Ray, who, as well as running the pub also used the building as a doctor's surgery. He later acquired the adjoining property and incorporated that into the inn. This double use of the building continued for more than one hundred years with no less than six surgeons selling ales and wine and operating a surgery. Two signs could be seen outside the inn, one showing the three hats of the cavaliers and the other with the owner's name and 'Surgeon and Apothecary' inscribed thereon.

In 1873 the then owner, Richard Bates, put in a tenant, one George Clatworthy, at a yearly rent of 22 pounds. From then on the 'Three Hats' had a succession of landlords and some years ago it was purchased by the Courage Brewery. The pub today is held on a twenty-year lease from the brewery and until recently mine host was Christopher Blondridge.

There were several other such watering holes built at that time, the 'White Hart' being one that is still a going concern and another was the 'Red Lion' which closed after fifty years. The 'George', also situated in the High Street was a very popular inn because it had stables where customers could be sure that their horses were well looked after.

10. THE TOWN

Some beautiful and interesting buildings in Milton date back to the sixteenth and seventeenth centuries. During the Georgian period, however, many of the buildings were given false fronts in brick, a material which first became popular for house building after the great fire of London. The house known as Jay's house is one such building; it stands next to two houses which are thought to be of the same age as Court Hall and built to house the gaolers.

Across the road from it a double fronted house was built in the eighteenth century for a Mr John Grayling who also owned the forge on the north side which was built during the reign of Charles I. This later became a farriery. On the wall of the house is an Invicta Fire badge; these badges were placed by insurance

Seventeenth century house, showing Invicta Fire Badge.

House built in the sixteenth century, now the Post Office.

companies who all ran their own fire brigades. If a brigade turned up at a fire in a building which did not have their badge on it then the unfortunate occupant would have to pay up before the fire was put out.

The Post Office occupies part of one seventeenth century house which was said to have been built 'high' for the drying of silk. This is a very beautiful and interesting house dating from the early 1600s although it has been altered during the twentieth century.

One building was known as Back's House because in the early seventeenth century it was owned by Humphrey Back. During the nineteenth century Back's House was home to the Jordan family who were plumbers and glaziers. One member of the family, Denham Jordan, however, was an author. He lived from 1834 to 1920 although he only spent the first twenty years of his life in Milton. He wrote 10 books, three under his own name, five under the name of 'A Son of the Marshes' and two anonymously. One called 'Annals of a Fishing Village' was about the Milton area although he called it Marshtown and Sittingbourne was referred to as Stanbeck. Another member of the family was Alfred Jordan who was the man who donated one of the Roman lead coffins to Maidstone museum in 1869. Bexhill (originally Backs Hill) lies behind the street where Back's House is situated.

Thomas Bradbury was a landowner and wool merchant whose wealth enabled him to build a house in Milton High Street, near the market. It was known as the Green House and had some notable features which included a trapdoor near the front door where any goods delivered could be put straight in the cellar. There were also places round the walls of the cellar where bees were kept in the winter and in the garden was an icehouse.

When Thomas Bradbury died, in 1601, he left four acres of land to the church. The profit from this gift was to be distributed among the poor of the parish on St Thomas's Day. This money was eventually used, in 1860, to build a row of almshouses near Court Hall, for 7 poor widows, on land which was part of the Butts.

The tall building on top of Milton Hill, number 60, was once the manor house and in the nineteenth century was known as Hinde's House. Here lived John Hinde with his daughter Eleanor. He was a man of many talents being Milton's coroner, clerk to the Milton Union, otherwise known as the workhouse, and Queenborough Town Clerk. He was also one of Milton's principal landowners. His daughter, who was jilted when younger, continued to live in the house after the death of her father and the story was told that as she grew older she became very eccentric and only ventured out at night to visit the churchyard. Some of the smaller children were afraid of her but the bigger ones tormented her by knocking on her door and running away. When she died she left some money for a fund to build almshouses for 4 poor persons in Cross Street.

Backs House, dating from the seventeenth century, photographed in 1999.

MEMORIES OF BARBARA WHITAKER

I remember a story about the Hinde House at the top of Milton Hill and about the white ghost of Milton. The story goes that the daughter of the house was jilted on her wedding day;

the wedding breakfast was all laid out and it is said that she was sitting there in all her wedding finery until she died. Some people said that they saw her ghost in Milton churchyard after that. It was said that the house was left open for a long time with the breakfast still laid out.

11. BRICKFIELDS

In the eighteenth century brickfields began to appear due to enormous quantities of brickearth, chalk and clays, containing sand and silt, being found in the area. The chalk was added to make the bricks yellow but one important ingredient had to be imported from London because ash was needed to complete the process as it was ignited during the firing of the bricks to bake them.

Thanks to the presence of these materials a new industry was born. By the 1860s there were brick fields all along both sides of the creek: Wills and Packham, Charles Burley and Smeed Dean were famous names in the trade with the latter being the second largest to the London Brick Company. Strictly speaking, a lot of these brickfields were in Sittingbourne although there were some in Milton, one was situated between the Wall and the Butts, and of course, men from Milton worked in all of them.

When Wills and Packham started their business a rule was made that no alcohol was to be sold in the brickfields and this rule was strictly enforced even though it was not at all popular with the workers. However, as a result of this the behaviour of the men was very much improved and people who lived in the area were thankful for it. A lot of the workers lived in tied cottages so that if they lost their jobs they also lost their homes.

The manufacture of bricks was a lengthy process. The brickearth was dug out in the winter and left in 'washbacks, layered between ash and chalk for as long as eighteen months, then it was put into pug mills where it was mixed. By the end of the nineteenth century these pug mills were driven by steam. Later, Wills and Packham became the first firm to power the pug mills by electricity. When the mixture was ready to be used brick sized pieces were taken to the moulder, the main craftsman of the team, who moulded the bricks. These were placed on a pallet before being loaded onto a barrow and taken to the drying sheds. Once they were ready to be baked the bricks were put into clamps by workers known as crowders. These clamps were fired by means of wood taken from the surrounding area. The primitive nature of the firing meant that the results were very uneven and therefore not all the bricks were of good quality and had to be sorted. The making of bricks involved many different stages and the men performing each stage were called: moulders, crowders, setters, temperers, offbearers and sorters.

This method of brick making lasted until the early 1900s, at which time the Milton Creek Conservatory Board imposed duties on all goods that used the creek for transportation. This meant that smaller firms had to close as they could not afford the charges. For the larger firms like Smeed Dean and Wills & Packham to survive a new method of brick making had to be found. A machine was introduced which could manufacture

A typical brickfield in the 1920's.

bricks faster and was less labour intensive and also a continuous kiln was brought in which meant that bricks could be made all year round.

By the 1920s the brick plant was producing 10,000 bricks an hour and a long kiln tunnel with cars inside that ran on tracks was in operation. This worked by one carload of bricks being pushed in at one end and a car coming out at the other end. Production was suspended for the duration of World War II and was started up again in 1946. It was ironic that by this time all the materials for brick making were brought in from outside the area, except for the ash, which in the old days had been the only ingredient imported. There was enough of that left locally from all the refuse that had been brought in from London during the previous century. This was just as well because with the widespread change from coal to central heating in homes there was no ash left to import. Wills and Packham closed in 1969 by which time there were just 50 people working for the firm. Smeed Dean continued to make bricks after this although the firm had become a part of A.P.C.M.

MEMORIES OF ERNEST CLARKE

I was born in 1911 and started work at thirteen; my first job was in the brickfields. Anyone who had a job to go to could leave school before they were fourteen. I lived about two and a half miles from the brickfield and I had to start work at 7 o'clock. We were allowed to stop work for breakfast at 8 o'clock but then we had to work through till 12 o'clock. Work started again at 1pm and finished at 5pm, no tea breaks in those days. We had to make forty thousand bricks a week in order to earn £2.10s. My job as 'the boy' was to load that number of bricks onto the barrow for that I earned 13 shillings. Although we didn't earn much money we were happy.

The boys who loaded the barrows were called flatheads by the men. There were shutters in the brickworks; the foreman said if we left them open all night we would get half a crown for it because it meant that we had to get up early and open them all again.

In the brickfields, as a boy, I worked for 26 weeks and spent 26 weeks on the dole because in the winter months there was only enough work for the men. This was in 1930 and for signing on the dole I received the grand sum of half a crown. This was means tested and we had to go to the Town Hall where we were interviewed by Councillor Wells. We were always asked, 'Have you been looking for work and how many times have you been to the pictures this week?'

I answered, 'I go twice a week.'

'How much do you pay?'

I told him tuppence.

'Now look,' he said. 'If you save all them tuppences up, look how much money you'd have.'

Out of my half crown I gave my mum 2 bob and kept a tanner.

MEMORIES OF RON SHEPHERD

When I left school I worked in brickfields, Wills and Packham, where the tramlines were, which is now part of St Michael's Road. It was a private road so it was shut off once a year. I was what was called a 'pushout'. We used to have to load a one-wheeled barrow. It was fifteen feet long and carried two rows of bricks, seventeen bricks, soft bricks, on each side on each palette. We would pick up the barrows and push them out to the huts, to dry out before they were brought back to the furnace to harden them. They used to bake them to make them into bricks. What they called cowls.

There was a man called Mr Turner who worked down the brickfields whose job was to dust the moulds so they called him the mole. They had to dust the moulds before they put the pug in. This man had a wooden leg and when it was cold the leather and wood used to rub together and squeak and you could hear him coming from half mile away as he walked down the tram road. When he was going home his leg never made a noise because it had got warmed up.

12. CEMENT

The manufacturing of cement had been taking place in the area since the nineteenth century. It was first made by extracting stone from the mud on the banks of the Swale, which was then layered with coal and burned in a bottle kiln. After it had cooled down horse mills were used to crush it into powder. By the second half of the 1800s George Smeed had become involved with the making of cement and although the procedure was the same the ingredients had changed. Chalk and mud were mixed together, the chalk coming from Highsted and the mud from the islands at the mouth of the creek.

The mixture was put into washmills where it was mixed with water. This was later drained and dried before being layered with the coal and put in the kilns which had under floor tunnels where wood was placed and lit to bake the contents. The resulting clinker was then cooled and taken to the cement mill where it was ground. Although the cement works were not in Milton it provided much employment for the people living there.

MEMORIES OF ERNEST CLARKE

One winter time after leaving the brickfields my dad said, 'Look here, there's a job going for you down in the cement mill. It'll be 6d an hour, twelve hours a day.'

I did seventy four hours and for that I received 30 odd shillings a week, after stoppages. Another chap's job was loading cement. They never used to wear socks in those days; they used to bind their feet with cloth called toerags and wear lace up shoes. As this man was going home one night you could see that all the blood was coming out of the lace holes, where he had been sluicing about in the cement (smack). It was hard work! I wouldn't want it again but I was happier then than I am now.

★ ★ ★

In the early 1900s other countries began to manufacture

cement, namely America, Germany and Belgium. This, of course, affected all the cement works in the country and many had to close. Others amalgamated to form A.P.C.M. Associated Portland Cement Manufacturers. The Smeed Dean Cement Works managed to remain independent until 1924 and, along with the Burleys, the Dolphin Works had a reputation for being the best in the world.

13. THE PAPER MILL

Although there was some evidence of paper manufacturing during the eighteenth and early nineteenth centuries it was in 1863 that something happened which was to change the face of Milton forever. This was the coming of Lloyd's Paper Mill. Edward Lloyd, who owned a mill in Boxbridge, on the outskirts of London, purchased the one owned by Edward Smith, which had closed in 1851. Towards the end of that year the mill was destroyed by fire and a new bigger one was built close to the site of the old one but nearer the railway line.

The building was started in 1866 and took about three years to complete. The mill was very much a family firm; on the death of Edward Lloyd it passed to his son Frank. It is thought that up to seventeen streets in Milton were demolished to make room for the new mill but others were built later to house the workers.

In 1871 it was still quite a small operation with only seven people working there but ten years later records show that the workforce had increased to forty eight. Fire was the greatest enemy of the mill, there being a large one in 1882, when the mill had to be rebuilt and another, smaller one in 1883. By this time about four hundred tons of coal and eighty tons of straw were being used every week in the construction of paper. Over the next ten years the mill grew with larger machines being installed, the building of a new boiler house and a chimney 170 feet high.

The Paper Mill, now owned by UK Paper.

Lloyd's Mill was always at the head of new developments and at the beginning of the twentieth century reports appeared in the trade papers, making the mill national news. By 1910 there were 16 machines installed and a year later the company Edward Lloyd Ltd. was formed comprising of the Sittingbourne Mill, one in Norway, pulp mills and a wholesale and export business which was based in London and it had branches all over the world.

The company expanded further when around 1912 it decided to build a dock at Ridham, on the north side of Milton Regis, which would be big enough to hold an ocean going ship. The mill and the dock were connected by a light gauge steam railway, which was made of reinforced concrete and was 2,805 feet in length. A bridge took it over The Wall and from there it ran beside Gas Road and across Cooks Lane. The presence of the mill was not in itself the reason why Milton changed; it was because the mill needed to use a vast amount of water to make paper, taking it from the creek itself and also from the surrounding area causing the streams to eventually dry up.

By 1920 the demand for paper had increased enormously and even though a three-shift system was started the mill could not compete with the demand. Because Milton was a built up area there was no room for expansion on the site and so another mill was built at Kemsley. This was a large edifice, made of bricks manufactured locally, concrete and steel and was finished in 1924. A grinder house was built next to the main entrance, which was connected to Ridham Dock by an aerial ropeway made of steel. This was used to carry logs for grinding.

MEMORIES OF RON SHEPHERD

I worked in the mill for 41 years and in that time I saw a lot of changes. There used to be lines of buckets going overhead; people today complain about noise, it's nothing compared with what it used to be then. Big iron buckets with handles on wires reaching from Ridham Dock to the mill. They used to carry logs which were dropped in piles about 90 feet high, you should have heard the noise they made. No one complained in those days, it was a different kind of noise.

★ ★ ★

Two paper making machines were installed which were the largest in the country, being 225 inches wide and when operated to their fullest extent ran at 900 feet per minute. A third machine was in the process of being built in 1927 when Frank Lloyd died. The water needed to operate the mill came from the Meads; it was pumped into large concrete ponds and from there into the water tower which was seventy feet high. By this time there were about 2,000 people working in the two mills and Frank Lloyd had decided to create a village in Kemsley to house the workers. He lived long enough to see the first of 750 houses built.

The businesses were sold to Sir William Berry whose family owned Allied Newspapers although the mills kept the name Lloyds. In 1936 the mills joined forces with Bowater's and Bowater Lloyd became the largest operation in Europe and the estimated half a million tons of newsprint they made was more than half of the total made in the United Kingdom. Because of the restrictions on the manufacture of newsprint during the war Sittingbourne Mill turned out other products, mostly containers for ammunition, made from Kraft liner boards.

MEMORIES OF GEORGE WICKENS

I started work in Sittingbourne Mill on 27th August 1946 and at that time there were between 5,000 and 6,000 people, men and women, working in the two mills. Women were employed there, initially, to replace the men who had been called up and they did various jobs, one of which was to make petrol tanks for aircraft; these were called drop tanks. They also sorted paper, did packing of reams and reels and worked as paper testers. When I started there were eight papermaking machines working and there was also a small one in what was called the old mill which made pulp for the others. These were numbered from ten to seventeen with half being upstairs. The machines were manned by a team of workers, the highest being called the Machineman; then came in order the Dryer, Spare Dryer, First Boy, Second Boy and the lowest was Press Boy. My first job was as Press Boy on number ten which made white paper. I remember that number 14 made straw paper, the straw was brought up from the wharf by conveyor belt and travelled over the bridge at New Road and was soaked in large tanks of acid before being used on the machine.

Number fifteen made Brown Sack Kraft, number sixteen made Kraft liner board and at the time I started work number seventeen made newsprint although it changed to Brown Kraft before eventually being turned over to white board which was used to make milk cartons and computer paper. Each machine had its own calenders, reelers and packers and the finished product was sent out in the mill's own delivery lorries.

There was also the wharf area which was part of the mill's business where the barges used to come and go loaded with pulp and coal which the mill used in its boilers, for power and steam. A steam engine brought the loads to the mill and this was used to take the men to work at Kemsley, day and night.

Many other tradesmen worked for the mill including:

Pattern Makers, welders, blacksmiths, painters, carpenters, fitters, rope makers, foundry men and barge repairers. They even had their own fire engine and firemen. Sittingbourne Mill had its own ambulance station with nurses on duty twenty-four hours a day.

Many people spent their whole lives working in the mill which, of course, was the normal thing in those days. They were looked after by the bosses; houses were built for the workers in Milton and in Kemsley too, where they had a clubhouse as well as cricket and football fields. In 1930 the Memorial Hospital in Bell Road was opened, this was a gift to the town by the Lloyd family in memory of Mrs Frank Lloyd and a club house for the workers was also built. This is in the Avenue of Remembrance in Sittingbourne.

Although I live in Australia now I still keep in touch with friends at home and they tell me that there are only about 400 people working in the mill now.

14. NON CONFORMIST CHURCHES

Up until the late 1700s there was only the Anglican Church in Milton, therefore people had no choice of worship. Then came a succession of non-conformist churches, the oldest of these being the Methodists. There seem to have been different

Bethel Mission Hall, St. Paul's Street. Now demolished

kinds of these with the Weslyan Methodists having a place of worship in Church Street and the Primitive Methodists building a Mission Hall in St Paul's Street. Other denominations in Milton were the Salvation Army in Bridge Street and Kingsmill Road and the Baptists in Flushing Street.

THE CONGREGATIONAL CHURCH

The arrival of the Reverend Thomas Wills started the non-conformist movement in Milton when he came to the town. He was of the Congregational Church and he preached in a room near the quay in a street once known as the Forge but which was later to become King Street. By 1790 a chapel had been erected in Crown Road which was a simple square building - cottage like with shutters at the windows. This opened officially on 8th August 1792 and was known as Paradise Chapel. The first minister was the Reverend Christopher Muston. The chapel was either rebuilt or enlarged in 1814 because there were by now 140 children in the Sunday school. A young preacher named Alexander Mills was largely responsible for the success of the church at this time but unfortunately he was drowned in 1816 in a boating accident on the River Medway.

Paradise Place, site of first Congregational Chapel

In 1840 there was some talk of them merging with the Sittingbourne chapel but this fell through due to the fact that they could not agree on which chapel to use. The congregation kept on growing with people coming from the Church of England to join in.

On October 3rd 1841 the Reverend Will Parrett began his ministry and the Paradise Chapel became even more popular with the people. The land on which it stood was purchased, the chapel was enlarged and a schoolroom was opened in 1843. Five years after this, part of the land was sold and the row of cottages called Paradise Place was built. This year also saw the building of a new Manse for the Minister.

There was a church rate levied on non-conformist chapels to support the Church of England and in 1856 William Parrett had his household goods seized for not paying this rate. Although he only owed three shillings and sixpence the property taken was worth six pounds. The goods were to be auctioned at the George Inn and the Reverend J Moss, Vicar of the Holy Trinity Church in Milton, said that he would buy all the goods and requested that no one should bid against him. After he had bought the property he handed it all back to the Reverend Parrett. He then passed his hat round and raised enough money to cover the debt and all the expenses, the auctioneer being the first to make a contribution. It is quite likely that Mr Parrett was the last person in England who was penalised for the non-payment of the Church Rate as it was abolished soon after.

Four years later a new church was built in Crown Road on the corner of Beechwood Avenue at a cost of £1,247 and this was paid for within a year. In 1865 the spire was built and also a new vestry and schoolroom were added.

Reverend William Parrett was the minister for 26 years and during his ministry the Congregational Church grew and prospered. On his 25th anniversary, in 1866, the church presented him with an illuminated address and 50 guineas. Unfortunately, he had to resign the following year due to ill health. He died in Gravesend in 1877.

The church continued to grow and in 1880 the schoolrooms had to be made larger again and a new organ was purchased. In 1894 there was a rift amongst the church members and some went to worship, firstly in the old Methodist building and then into a new Bethel mission hall in Church Road. Luckily, in 1909 they were united again. The church continued to be used as a place of worship for many years until the building was closed in the 1970s and Milton and Sittingbourne churches amalgamated, one hundred and thirty years after this move was first suggested. It was deconsecrated and used by a local scout group, finally being demolished in 1992.

*Congregational Church, Crown Road.
Now demolished and replaced by houses.*

It is not known when the burial ground was opened but it is thought that the first person buried there was Charles Henry, aged eight, the son of the Reverend William Parrett. He was buried under the apple tree.

From the *EAST KENT GAZETTE* *JANUARY 1998*

Permission was granted for the building of houses on the land previously contaning the Congregational Church and the graveyard. Unfortunately, the building started before the bodies had been exhumed and removed to Sittingbourne Churchyard. It was said that the building was only taking place on the chapel site but Mrs Glennys Pearson of Milton Regis, who has ten ancestors buried there, said that workmen had piled rubble on the graveyard and trundled machinery over it. One of the remaining gravestones has been donated to the Dolphin Barge museum as it belonged to an important barge builder of the 1800s. One small headstone, marked C P H 1846, is believed to be that of Charles Henry Parrett aged 8, son of Reverend William Parrett, who came to Milton in 1841 and was responsible for the raising of funds to build the Congregational Church to replace the little Paradise Chapel. The money raised came from local people who gave their hard-earned money to the cause even though none had much to spare.

Of the people buried in the churchyard 54 were children, 39 were under 1 year with the youngest being just 30 seconds old. All the bodies (all 400 of them) were re-interred in Sittingbourne Cemetery in a grave measuring 8ft wide, 7ft long and 9ft deep in the middle of a large flower bed near the entrance.

THE MEMORIAL

In October 1999 a service was held to dedicate a stone in memory of all the people who had been buried in the Congregational Churchyard. The Mayor of Swale, Councilllor Ann McLean and a number of people who had ancestors buried there attended the very moving ceremony which was conducted by the Reverend John Titlow, minister of Sittingbourne Congregational Church. The major part of the cost of £1,000 was donated by the funeral directors, High and Sons of Sittingbourne. The service was held at the new part of the cemetery in Capel Road.

15. THE WORKHOUSE

The Poor Law Amendment Act led to the building of Milton Union Workhouse in North Street. This act was designed to discourage idleness among the poor and instead of supporting destitute families and the infirm in their own homes the people concerned were sent to the workhouse where families were split up. Life was so hard that everyone tried to avoid going there.

Before the advent of the workhouse in the 18th century the poor were the responsibility of the Parish in which they lived and the payments were in the charge of the Churchwardens. Milton account books show that payments were made to widows living in their homes as well as to almshouses. Money for repairs to houses was also made. Those who were sick or died were also taken care of by the Parish. One such lady in 1674 was given 9 shillings, her nurse, goodwife May received the sum of 4 shillings to look after her, and when she died the four men who carried her to church shared 4 shillings and fourpence and the person who buried her earned 2 shillings. As well as looking after widows and the elderly sometimes the Parish would pay for a young person to be apprenticed. In 1676 one man was paid to take a young girl as his apprentice and she was allowed 8 shillings and 4 pennies for clothes. Young people were also given money to have their hair cut.

Occasional payments were also made to people in need, such as sailors shipwrecked in a storm and also to people who lost their possessions due to storms. At one time a sum of 3 shillings was paid to a woman for looking after a condemned man and for providing him with candles and other necessities. At the beginning of the 18th century Milton faced the problem of people coming into the town and needing help and it was quite usual to pay people to leave the area.

In 1722 the Poor Relief Act came into force and in 1724 the house of Richard Fox became the workhouse. This workhouse remained for more than one hundred years during which time many items were bought for the benefit of the inmates including things like spinning wheels, saucepans, a porridge pot as well as meat, turnips, cheese, milk and other necessities of life. Those living there also needed to have clothes bought, their shoes were mended and the men shaved. The inmates were expected to work and as well as doing rough menial tasks were taught various trades such as weaving. The children were educated; records show that in 1773 a woman was paid 19 shillings and 3 pennies to teach them. A Cat-of-Nine tails was purchased in 1786 for the purpose of punishing wrongdoers. It was a very hard life for anyone unlucky enough to find themselves in the workhouse but there were a few treats. They received a few pennies to spend at the Whitsuntide fair and also money for a Christmas present. Although the poor cost the Parish quite a lot the work they did made some money; records show income for work done by the poor.

Courtesy of Court Hall Museum

The workhouse at turn of century, later a hospital.

As time went by the rules became stricter and life was even harder. In 1817 a rule was passed that although all the inmates should have warm clothing of good quality they should be dressed alike which meant, of course, that they were easily recognisable wherever they went. It was decided, in 1820, that in future everyone should be given meat with their dinner on Sundays although it is hard to understand whether this was an improvement or not. A typical week's menu of the times was: breakfast, six ounces of bread and half an ounce of cheese. For the main meal: four days a week bread and cheese, two days suet pudding and vegetables and on Sundays meat pudding and vegetables. The elderly were given milk and tea and children had milk twice a day. When they were sick the elderly were allowed half a pint of porter a day. They had to eat with spoons as there were no knives and forks. Although there was very little cutlery money was spent to provide spittoons for the men. By 1839 the inmates were also given a Christmas dinner. Later someone was given the job of waiting at the gate to ensure that the children all went to school together and all those who worked went out at the proper time. If anyone returned later than 6.30pm they went without supper and all those who didn't want supper had to be back by 8.00pm.

There were people supported by the Parish even though they did not live in the workhouse and their lives became harder, too. In 1823 relief was stopped for anyone keeping a dog and ten years later illegitimate children were no longer supported. All those on relief were encouraged to find work and in times of unemployment were induced to go to a new area. To help people accept this offer a fund was introduced in 1841 to pay their expenses.

In 1834 a new Poor Law Act was passed and commissioners were appointed to oversee the building of new workhouses. A meeting was held in the old workhouse in 1835 at which Sir Francis Head, the Assistant Commissioner for Kent, told all the representatives of the 18 parishes that made up the Milton Union that the Central Poor Law Board would support them if the poor objected to the new provisions. And object they did! The poor who wanted the financial help to continue took action in support of this by rioting and by locking the local magistrate in the Rose Inn in Sittingbourne. The riots only stopped when the soldiers sent for from Chatham threatened to open fire.

Once the disturbances were over, land was purchased and the new workhouse was built next to the old one. The people were divided into three groups, the old and sick, the able-bodied men and women and children. Young married couples were allowed to live together providing they behaved themselves, because although the workhouse had to be made as unpleasant as possible it was felt that poverty should not be regarded as a crime. Despite this, when couples with children went in there the children were not allowed to sleep or eat with their parents.

Older people feared the workhouse and would say to their families, 'Don't let me end up in the Spike,' the local term for the place and it became a kind of bogeyman to the children of the poor. 'Behave yourselves and work hard or you will end up in there', was the cry in many homes. Of course, most of the people who were unfortunate enough to enter the place were not there because of anything they had done wrong. They were victims of circumstance, being left without the means to earn a living due to old age, unemployment, sickness and widowhood. No Welfare State in those days!

According to the 1841 census there were 128 inmates: the eldest being a man of 90 and the youngest a baby who was 9 days old. Of the 128, 55 were children under 14 and only 22 were over 65. By 1851, there was a Governor as well as a Matron, teacher, cook and a porter living in the workhouse along with 107 inmates, partly because there was a smaller number of children. By 1881 there were 142 people, including 36 students.

Another view of workhouse, now a housing estate.

All the residents were expected to work but efforts were made to lighten the burden at Christmas when treats would be provided. They would be given plum pudding, with the men receiving tobacco, the women tea and sugar and the children were given fruit. At a meeting of the Board of Governors in 1898 conditions in the workhouse were discussed and the Chairman refused a request for the men to be given tea the same as the women were. He said that most inmates were given tea by their friends. A request for everyone to be allowed to have visitors on Sundays was also discussed but it was decided that each application should be considered individually by the Master.

By the beginning of the twentieth century the number of poor people had dropped, partly because of the introduction of the old age pension before the first world war. This was five shillings a week for all those over 70 years of age. Then came the introduction of National Health Insurance which also helped to make people more independent.

As time went by the workhouse became known as Milton Almshouse and as the unemployed began to receive help from other sources the building eventually became used more and more as a hospital. In 1964 the National Health Service took control until the hospital was closed in 1990 when it was demolished to make room for housing.

16. SCHOOLS

By the time that the first education act came into force in 1870 the church had been running schools for children in Milton for nearly fifty years. The first one opened in 1821; it was called the National School and Mr Hinde, who was clerk to the governors, asked all parents to send their children to school 'clean skinned and short haired'. In 1848 the Elementary Schools were built on the site and these were run as an infants' and a mixed junior school. There was also a private school for boys run by a Mr Grigsby at his home at The Wall. However, there were far more children in the area than there were places for them at the schools and the education act sought to remedy that. The local people were not at all happy with the act's proposal to put up the rates to pay for new schools and the leading Methodists in Milton decided to enlarge the Sunday school building and use it as a day school.

In Sittingbourne the Church of England set up a committee to raise subscriptions for new schools to be built. It was felt that the children benefited more from church-run schools because of the religious teaching they received. The money raised was, however, found to be insufficient for the number of children concerned and in 1875 the Milton School Board was set up to take over the running of the Butts School.

New laws came into force in 1877 that stated that education was compulsory for all children between the ages of five and thirteen. This caused problems in Milton as teachers were refusing to admit children from poorer families, and there were many of them. The grants that the schools were given depended very much on examination results and so the brighter the children the more money the schools received. As the poorer children were mainly the offspring of parents who themselves could not read or write they arrived at school not knowing their alphabet and so the chance of them passing exams was small. In 1879 a final notice from the government was issued to the effect that places had to be found for all children and in 1898 the boys at the Butts School moved into a new building.

By the 1890s all the schools were reporting poor attendance and bad behaviour. The attendance levels could be explained by the fact that children used to work. The school used to stay open in August and the children had their summer holidays in September so that they could help with the hop picking. Even so, many of the children had to work in the fields in August and October, mainly helping with the harvest and picking potatoes. Some boys were absent for the whole summer, working in the brickfields.

When all the children did attend, the classes were very large; as many as one hundred were taught by one teacher when there was a staff shortage. It was quite usual for older children, who were intelligent enough, to help with the teaching and the rules for them were very strict. They had to dress soberly and start early in the morning. The subjects taught were many and as they were church schools scripture was one of the most important. English, arithmetic, history, geography and dictation were also taught and the children wrote on slates which their parents had to provide.

The Butts Infants School, now called Milton Court Primary.

The Education Act of 1902 was introduced to help the brighter children from poor families to go on to further education thereby increasing their chances of getting better jobs. This act meant that in future education would be paid for out of the rates, which did not please the ratepayers at all. The non-conformist churchmen were also unhappy because as the Board Schools were run by the Church of England they felt that it was a case of taxation without representation.

MEMORIES OF MARGIE HEARNDEN

I started school in 1916 and I was often naughty and on these occasions I had to stand behind the blackboard and I would entertain the class by pulling faces. This used to have them in stitches. I said, one day, that a certain girl had fleas jumping all over her head and they took her away and cut off all her lovely long hair. I feel so ashamed when I remember that! Another girl I had in my sights was called Doris Cook. I knocked her out once and my poor old mum had to pay the doctor's bill. I got into real trouble for that one.

★ ★ ★

During the First World War school life carried on as usual apart from one or two interruptions, one being the cancellation of the Whitsun holiday in 1916. To celebrate the signing of the peace treaty, at the end of the war, the children marched through the town to the recreation ground on July 7th 1919. There they enjoyed an afternoon of sports followed by a gala tea.

In November 1934 a day off school was granted so that everyone could join in the celebration of the wedding of the Duke of Kent to Princess Marina. By 1939, however the war clouds had gathered again and shelters had been built to protect the children from possible air raids. On May 8th 1945 the children had two days off to celebrate the end of the war. A sign at the school read, 'TODAY V.E. DAY TOMORROW CLOSED.'

MEMORIES OF BOB WHITAKER

I went to the Butts school and when I was 11, in 1937, I took part in a competitive exam for the whole district to try for a place at Borden Grammar. I passed with two of my mates, Mickey Gordon and Peter Bowles. They were so proud of us at the Butts School that they put our names on the Honours Board in 1938.

At the Butts we used to have outings once a year and these were paid for by collecting jam jars and rabbit skins and we went to places like the Tower of London, London Zoo and the Science Museum. I saw a photograph of Milton School not long ago, there was a gap between two class rooms, about six feet wide, and the whole area was covered in jam jars.

MEMORIES OF BARBARA WHITAKER

On Empire Day we used to wear our daisies; Miss Proctor used to play the piano and we sang 'Jerusalem'. One girl would be chosen to dress up as 'Britannia' for the pageant. Right near the office of Miss Humphries (the Head Mistress) was a very narrow brick stairway that led to the stockroom. Here we used to go and get the pens and ink, which was in powder form. We brought it down and mixed it with water.

We got a third of a pint of milk free. In the winter this was so cold that we stood it on the radiators to warm it up and in the summer it was boiled to stop it going off. It did not improve the taste! The pupils were divided into three houses; Rowena which was green, Pilgrims, blue and Maid of Kent, red. We wore badges and we received points for doing good work.

★ ★ ★

One of the teachers at the school in the late forties and early fifties was called Ethel Dewberry who began her teaching career later in life. She started out as a teacher's assistant in 1948 but in 1949 did a year's training course and became qualified to teach infants. Her special subjects included art, music and craft.

MEMORIES OF DON KINGSNORTH

All the lads from the bottom half of Charlotte Street went to the Butts School and we remained friends for all the time we were there. There were Sam Jefferies, Bobby Adams, Bob Fuller and his brother Bert, Porky Wheeler, Bobby Miles, George Bolton and Brian Mills and one friend who lived down in the heart of Milton, Jimmy Cornelius. The school was situated at the Butts, behind Sprottshill. It was a lovely old school and Mr Coupland, the headmaster, who was a tall upright man, commanded respect although he was very fair. One time when the playground was frozen over some of the children had started a long slide across the playing area. He came out and had a couple of goes before restarting lessons. One of the lessons during the war years was gardening. We were all encouraged, as was everyone in the country, to grow vegetables. This was done on a plot of land near the school and we were told that we were 'Digging For Victory'.

MEMORIES OF MORRIS LEWRY

I was born in Bassett Road, which is actually in Sittingbourne, in 1937. We moved to Springfield Road, in Milton, and I went to school at the Butts. My headmaster was Mr Coupland. We always knew him as Joe although his initial was E. There was a wonderful master there called Mr Bert Furlow; he was in the First World War and his favourite story began: "When I was in Mesopotania....." and if we didn't want to learn anything we could easily set him off on one of his favourite books. If we were very good he would read to us from 'Wind in the Willows'. As he read he lived every part, if only there had been tape recorders about at the time it would have been great. The other story he often told us was 'Treasure Island'. I still have a great love for those two stories.

The one outstanding thing about Mr Coupland was that he was very strict. If we did anything wrong he sent for us to go to his office. After giving us a telling off he would send us to the cupboard in the corner to choose whichever cane we liked, which was rather frightening.

I was there during the wars years and left in 1944. When I left school I went to work in a gents' hairdressers. While I was at the Butts we spent a lot of time in the air raid shelters and as far as I know they are still there, under the pavements. In 1995 I toured round the school and the classrooms looked exactly as I remembered.

MEMORIES OF VALERIE HEARNDEN

I was born Valerie Cornelius at number 17 Bridge Street and I was one of six children. Among my earliest memories was one when I attended the Butts School, where the teachers left a lasting impression on me. The one called Mrs Naves terrified me. I used to play hookey whenever I could just to avoid her, until my mother marched me back to school. Mrs Bennett, the headteacher, always assured me that I had nothing to fear if I was a good girl and behaved myself. I always thought I did anyway. I remember Mrs Connelly too, she took a particular dislike to a pupil named Ann Carpenter, who after having her knuckles rapped used to jump at the teacher and claw her hands and face. For this she was sent home. Adjoining the school but standing in its own grounds was a house called Langley House. It was part of the school and the children were allowed in to tend a patch of garden. We were always a bit wary of going inside the house as people said it was haunted and we were convinced it was.

★ ★ ★

Although the Butts school was the biggest in Milton there were other schools in the area. A couple of them were small private schools and there was an infant's school at Grovehurst and St Paul's Infants in Church Street.

*Peter Mantle and fellow pupils at
St. Paul's Infants School, Church Street*

MEMORIES OF PETER MANTLE

I went to the Holy Trinity School in Church Street. At lunchtime we would go along the tram road that used to run alongside the railway down by the brickfields which was not far from the school. We often played in the 'poke', this was clay from the brickfields, and got very dirty and the headmaster, whose name was Mr Catt, would line us up and inspect our hands and nails because he knew where we had been and he would say to me while rapping my knuckles on the desk, 'For your punishment, Mantle, you can go and get me 20 Players Airmen cigarettes.'

This was in the early fifties. Although it was illegal for children to buy cigarettes the shopkeeper knew what we were doing and who sent us. The 'poke' was in big concrete vats the size of a swimming pool and it was said that if you fell in you would be sucked under and there were stories going round about people who did die, but I don't know of any cases.

There was a little bit of an upset at home because we knew that my pals were not going to pass the eleven plus. They were going to the new school called Westlands and so I made sure that I wasn't going to pass it either. My father passed for the grammar school when he was a boy but his family couldn't afford for him to go. He was very angry when he found out that I had put crosses and lines on my exam paper. After a very average education at Sittingbourne West, boys and girls were taught separately, I went for an apprenticeship. I had to go to college, which was a lonely environment because my mates weren't with me. It was a great surprise to me when I swept the board. It was so easy for me, and one subject, I can't recall which one, was marked for presentation and neatness, and I got 100%. This was the first time that this had happened in the history of the college.

They wanted me to become a full time mature student and sit a test examination to go to the City of London University to do a course in mechanical engineering. This would have meant doing five years intensive study so I chose to buy a motor bike and get married instead. I don't know if my dad ever forgave me but we remained pals.

★ ★ ★

During the first half of the twentieth century education for the working classes improved considerably. Examinations were introduced that allowed bright children to go to the local grammar schools in Sittingbourne. Once at the grammar schools the children were able to study for and sit the School Certificate. By 1951 this exam became the General Certificate of Education (GCE) and was held at Ordinary and Advanced levels. Pupils from all walks of life were now able to compete on equal terms for places at University and have careers.

Book Two

Milton in the 19th Century

1. THE TOWN

In 1804 life in Milton changed a little for the better with the Improvement Act. It was from this date Improvement Commissioners met regularly in Court Hall to discuss provisions for the 'paving, cleansing, lighting and watching of the streets, lanes and other public places...and for the removing and preventing of encroachments, nuisances and annoyances therein'. To this end a Surveyor and Inspector of Nuisances was employed to see that the work was done. A second act was passed in 1838 that reinforced the first one and among the regulations was one which stated that 'the watchmen were not to be harboured by publicans' and another that 'writing on walls was prohibited'. Rates were levied on the local residents for the first time to pay for all these improvements and also for the installation of gas mains and sewers. Milton Gasworks was built in 1836 at a cost of £2,000. During the same year street lights, powered by gas, were introduced to the town. The gasworks was a public company and the profits were used to help alleviate the rates.

By 1858 the streets of the town had some pavements, although there was still much to be done, and all the street lighting had been installed. However, there were still no public sewers and the effluence from houses and the primitive toilets often overflowed from the cesspools into the streets causing fever and ague.

Sickness and disease were very prevalent and the most deadly was cholera. Milton, like the other Kentish ports had, in the 1830s, imposed strict quarantine laws on ships entering the creek from abroad but this did not prevent, in 1849, an outbreak of the disease which started in Rainham and spread to the surrounding villages. Another large outbreak occurred in 1854 and the local people tried various remedies, including the burning of tar barrels.

The situation was not helped by refuse being brought in by the barges from houses and stables in London. It was delivered to the Parish Wharf, not surprisingly nicknamed Dung Wharf by the local people. This cargo was used by local farmers along with sprats and starfish to fertilise their fields and as the area was very low lying it was often flooded. This wharf was one of the infamous 'Seven Stinks' of Milton. The other six were: the creek itself, the tannery, the gasworks, the sewage works, the fellmongers and a firm that made tallow candles that was owned by the Budds family. They lived in Middletune House which is the building situated where the High Street meets Crown Road.

Middletune House, home of the Budds family in the 18th century.

By the 1860s a sewer had been built but it flowed into the creek and as a number of people still drew their water from this it wasn't much help. There were many disputes over water supplies between Milton and neighbouring Sittingbourne as the latter owned the water works at Keycol and when Milton asked to buy half, their request was turned down. It took a commission to sort out the problem and it was decided that although the towns should stay separate on this issue, a way was found to ensure that Milton's water supply would be maintained.

The Town Hall was built in 1803 to replace the market, which had stood in the middle of the road. The building contained committee rooms, anterooms and one for meetings and concerts. In 1887 a clock was erected to celebrate the Golden Jubilee of Queen Victoria and this clock used the original Milton Bell. The town changed from being a parish and head of the Milton Hundred in 1894 when a Local Government Act altered the Improvement Commissioners into Milton Urban District Council with 12 members. They were responsible for the sanitary arrangements among other things. Water was still obtained from Keycol Hill and gas from the council owned gas works.

All the houses built on the hill were, of course, safe from the tidal flow of the creek and were home to the people who had money but for the ordinary folk home was in the houses built

The Wall

further down the hill. During the 1840s Milton was described as a quaint old fishing village with many narrow streets which went down to the water's edge. As the population increased, due to the presence of the brickfield industry and the paper mill, more and more houses were built in this area, which was called Tubwell. All these homes were subject to much flooding. As well as the creek there were also two large holding ponds in the area and, of course, the streams that fed the creek. The inhabitants of the houses in streets such as Flushing Street, Mill Street, Bridge Street and The Wall were constantly having to dry out their homes; it was a way of life.

2. LOCAL INDUSTRIES

Milton Creek, as well as being an important waterway for shipping, was a hive of activity for other industries during the second half of the eighteenth century. Oyster dredging continued to be a very lucrative business; in 1851 the oyster beds in the Stangate area were owned by Mr Alston and those of the East Swale by Mr Hills. Altogether 140 freemen constituted the Company of Fishermen and Dredgers and between them they held the lease of all the oyster beds, which were situated at the junction of the creek and the Swale. For this right they paid the Lord of the Manor £100 and 4 bushels of oysters yearly.

The oyster season went from August to May and many of them were taken to Billingsgate; they were kept fresh by being immersed in salt water and fed on oatmeal. At Christmas time some of the oysters were carried round the farms and traded for turkeys and ducks and other seasonal goods. The oyster trade flourished until 1896 when a severe frost finished it completely.

Another resource that came from the creek was salt and there were more than 20 salt pits. The refining of salt was a fairly easy and cheap process and much of the end product was used to preserve meat and fish. This was very necessary for keeping food fresh especially for the men who earned their living by going to sea. Other businesses were also set up because of the creek; shops selling marine stores and sail makers being just two.

1869 saw the opening of the Milton Mineral Works where such delights as soda water, potassium water, hop ale, ginger beer and lemonade were made. In the same year Frederick Littlewood started his engineering works at the top of Milton Hill. His firm was responsible for fitting a steam engine to a windmill in 1888, which had been damaged in a storm twenty years before. This windmill was in an area of the town known as the Meads. Frederick Littlewood was also at one time the Chairman of Milton Urban District Council.

Meads Windmill at Vicarage Road.

One obvious source of employment was on the vessels that sailed the creek. The fleet of barges grew and the creek became even busier. There were always barges moving from quay to quay being loaded or unloaded with heavy cargoes. The children played at the creek side, which wasn't fenced off, and became used to the hustle and bustle. Many a boy had a yearning to work on the barges and if they were that way inclined it was difficult to dissuade them. They found the life hard but never boring; as well as having to cope with the cargoes of sand, cement, china clay, coal and bricks they also had the weather to contend with, which was at times very unfriendly. Most of them grew to love the life, which gave them a chance to sail and visit other places; they certainly didn't do it for the pay or the conditions because both were bad. It took years of hard work and experience to become a barge captain but those who made it entered a well-respected fraternity.

A barge at Milton Creek.

3. TRANSPORT

BARGES

In the nineteenth century the creek was the main source of transport. The owners of the brickfields also had their own boat building yards on the creek. The largest of these was owned by Smeed Dean but there were also some independent family firms. Robert Mark Shrubsall and Stephen and John Taylor were among the most familiar names. The Taylor family, who were also rope makers and owned a rope walk in Milton, built barges for nearly one hundred years; their business was taken over by Wills and Packham in 1889. The most popular vessel was the spritsail barge because it could carry enough bricks to build a house and by the middle of the century there were more than one hundred of them in use. In 1899 the Shrubsall yard was taken over by Eastwoods.

Besides having an interest in barges two operators, Thomas Mandark and John Huggens, each owned a hoy that ran a service to Beale's Wharf in London every two weeks. The hoys carried passengers as well as goods and were a regular service so that anyone who had business in London could be sure of reaching their destination on time. When John Huggens died, in the 1850s, most of his barges were bought by Smeed Dean. Paper, cement and bricks were the cargoes as well as produce from the farms and on the return trips they carried refuse and the ash necessary for the making of bricks. Not only was the capital a very profitable market for the selling of bricks but it also gave the barges a return cargo thereby increasing the profits of the owners. As the number of houses being built in London grew so did the population which in turn meant more ashes and sewage to bring back to Milton. When the railways opened there were those who still preferred to travel to London by the hoys which sailed from Milton Quay.

RAILWAYS

The coming of the railways had an enormous impact on the way of life for the people of Milton, as it did everywhere. 1858 saw the arrival of the first passenger trains that ran between Chatham and Faversham. The line between Sittingbourne and the Isle of Sheppey opened two years later. Although the trains made travelling very much easier for passengers there were complaints from the freight side of the business. Lack of space for the carts to get close to the rails was one and another was that the trains frightened the horses. Until the end of the century there were accidents, some very serious, but this was rectified by the introduction of a new points system. The London, Chatham and Dover Rail Company merged with South Eastern Railways at the end of the century.

4. THE FIRE BRIGADE

The first town Fire Brigade Station was in Crown Road. This was formed in 1884 and was made up of volunteers who were paid only when they were called out. The first Chief Officer was Mr Watson of 'The Coniston', London Road. To call out the fire brigade it was necessary to telephone Sittingbourne 62 or ring the alarm bell at the Town Hall. The firemen were summoned by the firing of a maroon rocket. The first man to arrive at the station had to fetch the two horses, which were housed in the field belonging to the George Inn, and then harness them to the Merryweather fire engine. The second to arrive was responsible for the lighting of the fire to get up enough steam to work the pumps. One can't help wondering if they ever arrived at the fire in time to stop the building burning down.

Fire Brigade outside Milton Town Hall in 1900.

In 1928 the premises were extended and renovated which meant that a fire engine purchased a year earlier could at last be housed there. It had proved to be too big to go in the old building. The Milton Regis fire brigade had used a manual pump for about 60 years. In 1939 it was renovated and stored in the parish church. The firm responsible for the work was the local firm of F. Littlewood & Sons. The fire pump, built in 1929, is now in a museum. Sittingbourne fire station opened in Crescent Street in 1897 and in 1930 the two brigades amalgamated.

Milton Fireman with one of the appliances.

5. SOCIAL LIFE

Although living conditions were very primitive for the workers, the men, especially, did not spend much time at home. They did, of course, work very long hours but there were certain activities on offer to fill their leisure time. Up until the latter part of the nineteenth century the main ones were politics and sport. The people who lived in the town were mainly Liberal, but the Conservatives always won the elections because the people from the very large rural area voted that way. During the run up to elections meetings were held which could be quite lively and on the day the voting took place in a meadow, as there were no polling stations. Sometimes there was quite a carnival air to the whole proceedings.

Bowls, of course, had played a large part in the sporting scene for many centuries but it wasn't until the second half of the nineteenth century that football, cricket, tennis, and athletics became popular sports in the town. The introduction of bicycles saw a formation of clubs in the area and water sports were popular, Milton Creek being the venue for swimming and rowing matches.

By the late nineteenth century there were many other pastimes on offer. As would be expected, during the Victorian era, the institutes and clubs that were formed were more for self-improvement than entertainment. There were lectures on literature, science, music and chess and although most of these were held in Sittingbourne, in 1876 Milton had its own institute. Its first concert was held a year later in the Assembly Rooms. The two towns joined together to form some clubs, one being the Sittingbourne and Milton Working Men's Club.

Although women would not have been allowed to become members of these clubs they were invited to parties and outings. The organisations had grand names such as: The Scientific Association, The Debating Society and the Mutual Improvement Society but the Society of Comical Fellows is an intriguing title. Was it formed for a serious purpose or just for the amusement of the members? All the well known organisations were around at that time, such as: the Oddfellows, the Order of Druids and the Ancient Orders of Buffaloes and Foresters. A new Foresters Hall was opened in the town in 1889.

For many of the ordinary workers, however, the pubs provided the main source of leisure. Of them there were many and they were frequented by both men and women. Surrounded as they were by poverty, squalor and sickness it was a way of escaping for a while and making their lives bearable.

6. THE COFFEE TAVERN

The large number of public houses in the area was causing a great deal of concern in the town and in order to combat the amount of drunkenness among the workers a coffee tavern was set up in January 1880 in a building at the bottom of Milton Hill. This was run by a band of non-conformists and was a place where men could go to play cards or chat; in short, to do the same things that they could do in pubs but drink coffee instead of beer. Coins are in existence which were tokens issued for the purchase of one penny worth of coffee and are dated 1880. The designs for the tavern were by Mr William Grant, a Sittingbourne architect, who also designed Kemsley Mill, Gore Court Pavilion and the swimming baths.

At the opening ceremony a letter was read out from the former Vicar of Milton, the Reverend W Harker, who had been

Bottom of Milton Hill around 1900. Coffee Tavern was in this area.

very involved in the founding of the tavern. He said in the letter that he hoped the tavern would become a haven for the promotion of health and social happiness. The new Vicar, the

Reverend Robert Payne-Smith said that it would check the national vice and sin of intemperance. It was agreed that notices should be put up asking people to sign the pledge although this would not be compulsory.

Although the tavern had been opened with high hopes of it providing a lasting place where men could meet and enjoy themselves without the presence of alcohol it survived only until February 1892. The main reason for this was the lack of money. Not enough shareholders had been found to keep it running or even to pay off the original building costs. During the eleven years that it was open the takings dropped from £600 for the year 1882 to £237 for the last year.

The demise of the coffee tavern meant that public houses such as 'the King's Arm's', which stood opposite the tavern and 'The Green Dragon' had very little competition and their reputation for being 'rough houses', where bottle fights on a Saturday night were taken for granted, were well earned.

7. THE PERIWINKLE

By the time the Periwinkle Stream had reached the creek it had already supplied water to the tannery and powered Kings, Mede and Periwinkle Mills. The latter had been in existence since the sixteenth century and worked up until the end of the nineteenth century. Its main purpose was to grind corn but there was a short period when pearl barley was produced. At the point where the stream flowed under Church Street it was about fifteen feet wide and a foot deep and where it emerged there was a cobbled ramp. Here horses would stop for a drink and elephants too, when the circus came to town; this must have been quite an event for the children.

8. ST PAULS CHURCH

Because of the stream and other springs many of the roads at the bottom of Milton Hill were swampy and subject to flooding. One of these roads was Water Lane so called for obvious reasons. Nevertheless, land there was given by the Archbishop of Canterbury for the building of a Chapel of Ease because so many people now lived in that area and therefore some distance away from the main church. It was felt that life would be easier for them if their place of worship were nearer. This church was built of brick with a nave, chancel, bays and an aisle. There was seating for about 500 people, 150 of which were free, and the church was lit by gas. On the day of the first service there was a procession through the streets with a hundred children carrying banners and flags.

9. THE TOWN

By the end of the nineteenth century the face of Milton had changed dramatically. The arrival of the railways coincided with the need for more houses due to the expansion of the paper mill and other industries. Roofing slates were one commodity that could be brought in by rail cheaply and easily and Charlotte Street is one street built this way. Crown Road also has very good examples of Victorian houses. This area was home to the Congregational Church as well as the fire brigade. Not far from there a large house was erected for Doctor James Crerar which was called Blair Park.

Typical Victorian House in Crown Road

With the mill and the brickfields providing more and more work, with improved sanitation and better housing the lives of some of the people who lived and worked there became easier. However, for others nothing seemed to change, their houses still flooded and their children still had to work to bring money into the home. The mill brought prosperity for some but for those who made their living from the creek things were very difficult. The effluence released into the water by the manufacture of the paper killed the fish and the men from about 90 fishing vessels found that their skills were no longer needed. In order to earn a living they either had to emigrate or work within the confines of the mill - not a happy experience for men who had spent their lives working in the open air.

'The White Horse'. The building was originally two of the houses in Charlotte Street which were built in the 19th Century to accommodate the workers employed by the ever exapanding Paper Mill.

As the town grew larger, expanding in all directions, it became difficult to tell where Milton ended and Sittingbourne began. Most of the local people would say, if asked, that Milton ended at the London Road although there are those who would choose the railway line as the boundary. By this time, however, the town stretched as far as Ufton Lane, William Street and Park Road. There is a plaque on the front of St Mary's Church in Park Road which places it in Milton. Part of The Wall, Hawthorn Road and Milton Road were actually in Sittingbourne which also complicated things.

The names of many streets changed: St Paul's Street was once Water Lane because it was often flooded and Love Lane became Mill Street, for obvious reasons. King Street was formerly Key Lane because it led to Milton Quay and Staplehurst Road was originally known as Blind Lane.

Book Three

Milton Regis in the 20th Century

1. THE FIRST DECADE

Throughout the early years of the 20th century things continued much the same for everyone. The paper mill continued to expand and flourish, as did the brickfields which meant that there was plenty of work. The pubs were still doing a roaring trade supplying beer and entertainment, not only to local people but also to those whose work on the barges brought them into the town. Change was in the air, though, and a suggestion was put forward that the towns of Milton and Sittingbourne should amalgamate. This was in 1902 but nothing came of it as the people of Milton voted to keep Milton for Miltonians.

By 1907 the Milton-Next-Sittingbourne Urban District Council was becoming increasingly frustrated by the post going astray. There were about twenty towns in the country called Milton which gave the Post Office many headaches as well. It was suggested at a council meeting that the name should be changed and various alternatives were put forward. After much discussion it was put to the vote and the name chosen was Milton Royal. The request was sent to Kent County Council and a few months later a reply was received from the Clerk of the Council to the effect that The Secretary of State was not able to advise his Majesty to agree to the name 'Royal' being used as the rules about using it were very strict. The council then asked if they could use the name 'Regis' meaning 'of or belonging to the King'. Eventually, Kent County Council granted the name change under the Local Government Act of 1894 S.55(3) and the town officially became Milton Regis.

Frank Lloyd started to build a dock capable of accommodating large ships in the Swale, north of Milton. These would bring the wood pulp necessary for papermaking and in 1907 a light railway was built to transport this wood pulp from Ridham Dock to the paper mill thus taking more traffic from the creek. This railway was also used to carry shift workers to the dock and later to Kemsley Mill.

*The Light Railway engine,
driven by Mr Mantle.*

MEMORIES OF PETER MANTLE

My dad worked on the Bowater's railway line; he worked shift work and one man who worked with him was a man who is better known these days for fund raising. His name is Dale Howting and for many years he has raised money for local charities. In those days he worked for the railway as a runner. The points had to be changed manually and it was Dale's job to jump off the engine as the train slowed down and run in front to change the points and then get back on the train.

I have on video a recording (transferred from cine film) of the last train that ran from Bowater's to Ridham Dock. My father was the driver and he drove the train from Sittingbourne to Kemsley with local dignitaries on board. It then became the Kemsley Light Railway.

★★★

By the end of the previous century the bargemen had formed a trade union and a strike in 1890 was followed by another in 1912. This was very bitter and led to Lloyd's no longer using barges on the creek; instead they used lighters and tugs. It was the beginning of the end for Milton Creek. The extraction of water by the mill and less barge traffic led to the creek silting up faster and the coming of the First World War speeded up the use of road and rail transport to carry freight.

2. THE FIRST WORLD WAR.

The summer of 1914 was being enjoyed by the people of Milton Regis with all the usual events taking place, such as flower shows and tennis tournaments, cricket matches and swimming galas. There was even talk of a cinema being built in the town but the declaration of war in August put an end to all such ideas.

Overnight the town changed. Although urged not to panic people rushed to buy large amounts of food, which only resulted in prices going up. Milton Regis became part of the war zone with armed guards patrolling the area. Troops began to arrive and were billeted in both Milton Regis and Sittingbourne. The first regiment to arrive in Milton Regis was the Royal Field Artillery and they were housed by local people who received 9d a night plus money for food. Those who took in officers were paid 3 shillings a night but they had to pay for their own food and stable owners were well recompensed for looking after the horses.

At the end of August there were advertisements to recruit men for the New Expeditionary Force and a new battalion of the 'Buffs' was raised. Enthusiasm for the cause was high with even the Boy Scouts joining in by helping to patrol the London Road. They also took part in a procession which started at Chalkwell and ended at the football ground. This was a rally designed to persuade recruits to join Lord Kitchener's Army. Also taking part were the Royal Field Artillery, the fire brigades from both towns and members of St Johns Ambulance Brigade. Many did join up, others who were reservists were called up and by October 350 men from Sittingbourne and Milton had been recruited.

With thoughts of their loved ones fighting in foreign lands always uppermost in their minds, nevertheless, the people made the best of their changing circumstances. Indeed, the presence of so many soldiers in the area was beneficial, especially to the local shopkeepers. Many fundraising events were organised and a Milton and District War Relief Committee was set up. By the end of the year matinees in local cinemas, whist drives, football matches and open-air concerts had taken place.

News came through from the front of local men being killed and wounded and a number of Belgian refugees were expected. Places in Sittingbourne were commandeered to take the wounded and G H Dean, of Bell Road offered to turn the house next to his home into a hospital for the duration. Meanwhile the town received a visit from King George V in the October and by the end of the year the troops that he reviewed had left and been replaced by the Royal Dublin Fusiliers.

By 1915 everyone was becoming more and more aware of the horrors of war. The 'Princess Irene' blew up in the Medway killing 78 dockyard workers, some of these being Milton men. The people were warned by Milton Urban District Council to stay indoors when there was an air raid and the gas was turned off at night to ensure that no lights were left on and to lessen the risk of explosions. The following month bombs dropped on Unity Street but no details were given out because of reporting restrictions. Some of the people went outside to have a look and saw the Zeppelins lit up by searchlights.

By this time security had been stepped up with night patrols and passes needed to visit the Isle of Sheppey. At this time too came the introduction of the National Register which meant that men in much needed skilled agricultural work would be exempt from being called up. This was of especial value to the area as there was a great shortage of farm workers and prices were rising all the time. At this time, also, the tax was increased on goods such as tea, coffee, cocoa, sugar and tobacco.

The news from the front was still the most important thing in everyone's mind and the Shrubsall family were devastated to learn that Reuben had been killed in the trenches. Others came home wounded and there was news of some being prisoners of war. A flag day and other fund raising schemes were set up to help these and local children helped by entertaining the wounded.

Ladies employed on Lloyd's Wharf during World War I.

As time went by Lloyd's Mill and the owners of the brickfields were anxious about the number of their employees who were being called up and they all applied for exemptions for their key workers. These were mostly granted. Women began to take the place of men in a number of occupations. They were to be found in the mill, on the farms and on the wharves, as well as in the more usual roles of nurses and cooks. Everything was now done for the war effort. Social life consisted of fund raising, there were restrictions on food and paper, suggestions were offered on how to prevent waste and everyone was urged to grow food which resulted in land being turned into allotments.

Troops in the First World War taking a break in Milton High Street.

In 1917 manpower was in short supply and campaigns to recruit more men for the forces were organised. The flow of traffic on Milton Creek had decreased due to a lack of crews and also because of the restrictions on all non-governmental activities. Although there were no bombing raids on Milton Regis at this time there were some not too far away and so sirens were installed in the mill and people were told to stay indoors when they heard the warnings.

A steady stream of news arrived from the front with letters containing details of battles and men coming home on leave. There was, of course, much sadness when news was received of men being reported dead or missing but relief for some whose husbands and sons came home wounded. One local man, George Kingsnorth (known as Don), who was serving in the Royal Army Medical Corps was awarded the Military Medal for bravery in the field.

*Military and Campaign medals won by George Kingsnorth
in the Great War*

The beginning of 1918 saw the introduction of food rationing with everyone receiving cards for meat and commodities such as butter and sugar. Now women were beginning to enjoy greater freedom. Although it meant that they had to work harder doing jobs like bricklaying and digging it also meant that they were able to join Trade Unions and take part in sports. They were, at last, given the right to vote and felt that they could now make a contribution to the affairs of the country.

As the war drew to a close and people thought that they could begin to relax the town was hit by an epidemic of influenza which resulted in the closure of the schools and other public places. This did not diminish the joy and excitement of everyone when the news broke of the signing of the armistice on the eleventh of November. The sirens sounded and the church bells rang out.

It was several months into the new year before the troops left the town and life started to get back to normal for the people of Milton Regis. There were those for whom life would never be the same again; the families who had lost loved ones or had them return home badly wounded. To celebrate the peace the people of Milton adorned the streets and their houses with flags and an archway was built and decorated at the entrance to the recreation ground. Here two thousand children and many adults were given tea after taking part in a parade through the town. Two years after the war ended the widows and children of all the Milton men killed in the war were given a special treat at Ufton Lane School. Entertainment and tea was laid on for them and the children were given presents of socks, stockings and sweets as well as a special commemorative mug.

3. THE 1920s AND 30s

As the horrors of the war receded a little from the minds of local people they tried to settle down and continue their lives as before. The pattern had changed, though, and adaptions to a new way of life had to be made. Men were coming home from the battlefields to find that their womenfolk had tasted new freedoms. The changing fashions with shorter skirts served to emphasise this and after doing men's jobs for a few years many women did not want to be chained to the kitchen any more. There was not enough work to go round and of course the men wanted and needed their jobs back. There were some new factories opening at this time. During the First World War a cherry factory was opened by F W Gooding to be followed by the one at Chalkwell road, belonging to Bennett Opie.

Having won the right to vote women started to take an interest in politics. By 1920 the Labour Party had begun to rise and Milton Regis had its first lady councillor. Other, lighter pastimes became popular. A Girl Guide company was started in the town and dancing classes were well attended. Carnivals were also very popular with many people taking part and visiting circuses added extra colour to the life of the town.

The building of the paper mill at Kemsley and the village to house the workers changed the landscape and more houses were built both in the town and in Sittingbourne to ease the overcrowding. One way the council tried to alleviate the situation was to encourage people to buy their own houses and they did this by offering to lend ninety per cent of the purchase price. In 1925 Milton Regis Urban District Council paid £150 for land that was used for farming, mostly in the form of orchards and this land was converted into a recreational ground. The drinking fountain, which was originally near to Court Hall, was placed in the ground.

In 1921 an event occurred that brightened the lives of local people. This was a visit to the town by Prince Albert, Duke of York; later to become King George VI. He came by road, first visiting the hospital at Keycol and he arrived in Milton Regis at about eleven o'clock stopping at the Town Hall in the High Street. It was a great occasion for the people and they turned out in force to welcome the Duke. Taking part in the ceremony were children from the Butts School, the girls dressed in white performed folk dances and the junior troop of boys paraded, wearing red jackets, white short trousers and blue hats. Afterwards the Duke was driven to Sittingbourne where he was greeted by town councillors and taken to see the paper mill and Burley's brickfield. He was then driven to Bell Road and had lunch in a pavilion. He was introduced to Mr and Mrs Dean and other local dignitaries before leaving the area.

There was another move to amalgamate Milton Regis and Sittingbourne but once again the Miltonians voted against it, this time with a smaller majority. Although they really wanted to keep their town separate it became increasingly obvious that, geographically, the two towns were already one and it seemed inevitable that they would, eventually, join together in every way. The boundary between them crossed streets and sometimes even houses and it was seen as a waste of money to have two lots of water and sewage works as well as the expense of running two Town Halls. The people of Milton Regis had to go into Sittingbourne to visit cinemas and to catch trains and, of course, many of them worked there, too. In 1929 Sittingbourne and Milton Urban District Council became a reality.

HRH Prince Albert, Duke of York pictured in the High Street in 1921

By the start of the 1930s electricity had been installed in the town but it was not put into the majority of the houses until much later. Buses became frequent sights and, although other, cheaper companies tried to set up in competition, Maidstone and District had the monopoly. In 1934 the Town Hall was pulled down and a few years later a library was built on the site. 1934 was also the year that a new Conservative Club was built in Church Street. The Member of Parliament for the whole of the 1930s and the war years was Mr Maitland, Conservative. He held office for seventeen years and when he resigned, Milton Regis had its first labour MP, Percy Wells.

Edward Littlewood, the owner of Littlewood's foundry in the 1930s, was a local councillor. He was very proud of Milton Regis and did not want the town to lose out when its council amalgamated with Sittingbourne's. When he heard there was a plan to re-thatch the roof on the sun lounge at the town's

The pavilion, on Recreation Ground, built in 1936, demolished in the 1950's

recreation ground he dreamed of having a similar building at Milton Regis. On their recreation ground there were only a few wooden benches for people to rest on and as the Silver Jubilee of George V's reign was drawing near he felt that a pavilion would make a nice memorial for this event. In May 1935 the council agreed that a plan, with an estimate of the cost, should be drawn up. Many months were to pass before the building was started as the plans had to be drawn and approved and the site had to be chosen. The building work finally began in June 1936 at a cost of £305. Edward Littlewood's dream of building a sun pavilion finally came true but he never saw it realised as he died before it was finished.

Celebrations were held to mark the Silver Jubilee of King George V and Queen Mary and these took the form of a parade, bonfires and a sports day. Two years later the town, like the rest of the country, was celebrating the coronation of another King, George VI, and this time the event was marked by street parties. Unfortunately, the weather was not favourable and these parties had to be held on different days.

MEMORIES OF GEORGE WICKENS

We had a party for the coronation of King George VI, it was held in Kingsmill Road and we were given coronation mugs and a new threepenny bit.

Street party in Kingsmill Road celebrating the Silver Jubilee of King George V.

Although the town's folk were used to coping with floods, in 1938 a sudden and terrible rain storm led to the rapid overflow of the creek and within minutes homes in the Bridge Street area had four feet of water in their living rooms. Public houses were also affected and the 'Watermans Arms', the 'Crown and Anchor' and the 'Kings Arms' had their cellars flooded and the beer ruined.

Lloyd's mills amalgamated with Bowater's in 1936 and business was booming, with more than 3,000 men being employed. Other firms, though, were feeling the pinch; builders in London and other places found that they could buy bricks cheaper from abroad than the ones made locally. In order to survive firms had to modernise, which meant using less labour.

Only five barges were built after the First World War, the last one in 1922 and these were subsequently fitted with engines. Smeed Dean had joined with other firms to form the Red Triangle Group, which in turn amalgamated with Blue Circle in 1931. This meant a loss of jobs for local men, as did the decision by Smeed Dean to sell off their fleet of barges. Bowater's took over both the Eastwoods and Sittingbourne Shipbuilding yards in the 1930s for the repairing of tugs and lighters. All the building yards were still in operation, although by this time it was mostly for repair work. The bargemen found that they were still needed, though, when the Second World War started.

4. THE SECOND WORLD WAR.

The fear of war against Germany was very real in 1938 and many plans began to be made for the safekeeping of the people. In Milton Regis, as in other places all over the country, the local paper gave instructions on how to build air raid shelters in gardens and it was proposed that trenches should be dug in different parts of the town for the protection of people on the streets. In October gas masks and respirators were issued, the latter were for babies and the air had to be pumped in by hand. These masks were ugly things and appeared quite frightening to children. At the end of the month, however, the Prime Minister,

Mr Chamberlain, returned from Germany with the paper that had been signed by Adolf Hitler and said that there would be no war. Everything calmed down and services of thanksgiving were held in all the churches.

Although life seemed to go on as usual during the first half of 1939 plans were still being made for the defence of the town. A voluntary service was set up to protect essential services and industries and an Air Raid Precaution Centre was organised. Young men were asked to register for training and others were called up for service. Plans had been made for evacuees to come to the town and though the general feeling was that war was inevitable everyone was still determined to enjoy the summer. All the sporting activities, flower shows and fetes went on as usual but were brought to an end on the 3rd September by the declaration of war against Germany.

MEMORIES OF BOB WHITAKER

My father and I went to the Congregational Church in Crown Road and we were sitting in there on Sunday September 3rd 1939 when the Reverend Father announced that we were at war with Germany.

'We will sing the National Anthem and take the collection,' he said, 'and then we will go home.'

As we came out of the church, walking along Chalkwell Road to Charlotte Street, the siren went and when we got home mum had laid all the gas masks out on the table. Our windows were boarded up with millboard, which was very thick. This was to stop the glass flying in an air raid. We had to pay particular attention at night to make sure that everything was blacked out and no lights showed.

MEMORIES OF DON KINGSNORTH

We moved to the bottom end of Charlotte Street, number 19, and my first real memory of living there was the declaration of World War II. I was playing in the street when a boy called

Bobby Miles told me that war was about to start. He was a couple of years older than I and I didn't understand what he meant. His words proved true when a few minutes later the siren started wailing and Bobby flew up the street as though his backside was on fire. It seemed to me as though that was 'it' as nothing else happened for a long time.

★ ★ ★

When the evacuated children arrived in the town they thought it was another world. Most had never seen the country side or fruit trees and they really enjoyed hop picking. Apart from a few air raid warnings, when shops closed and people used the shelters, nothing much happened for the next few months. Knitting and sewing parties were formed to make warm clothes for the local regiments and parcels of food were collected and sent out. As in the First World War fund raising activities were started. Blackout regulations were strictly enforced; air raid wardens would patrol the streets and anyone whose house was showing a light would be in serious trouble.

The schools were not allowed to open unless they had proper shelters for the children and teachers, who were given training in first aid. Trenches were dug, lined with concrete and covered. The Butts school had these shelters and the children continued their education even though some only went in for half days.

MEMORIES OF BARBARA WHITAKER

I remember when I went to the Butts in the war that we used to go for half days. There were air raid shelters and we used to take a tin and in it were a collapsible cup, an oxo cube, and some biscuits; it was an oxo tin, which was sealed with Elastoplast. That was taken into the shelter and if we were down there for any length of time we were allowed to open our tins. This happened twice. There was a supply of hot water in the shelters to make our oxo drinks with.

The bargemen who had begun to feel that there was not much left for them to do suddenly found that there was a role for them to play in the fight against the enemy. The barges were used to carry goods around the coast and for other war work, although the crews received no training and often sailed with only a couple of rifles on board.

MEMORIES OF BOB WHITAKER

Eddie Shrubsall, my great uncle, was extremely well known among the barging fraternity and in 1940 he invited me onto his next trip. Fred, my brother, already worked with him as Mate. I asked him where we were going and he answered 'Brightlingsea'. So, early one morning, we caught the workmen's train to London, which cost half a crown, and eventually found ourselves somewhere near Tower Bridge, where we picked up the barge. He had with him two sacks and we were going along this street with cobbled stones and went in some little shops. In the first shop he filled one sack with bread and in another he filled the second sack with provisions.

As the bread was stale we dampened it and dried it off in front of the stove. We passed the time on board by singing, 'Here we lay at Brightlingsea Bay, waiting for the wind to come our way---------'.

Uncle never swore and never drank anything but water except on rare occasions he would put a spoonful of 'sherbert' in a two-pint pot. That's as much as he had of beer. He hated rifles but Fred had one on board and when we popped it off (quite regularly) he went down below.

That night, when we moored off Southend, there was an air raid. The Germans used to come up that way and drop mines in the water in 1940.

★ ★ ★

Food rationing was introduced in 1940 and queues began to form outside shops. Campaigns to save money for the war effort raised more than £10,000 and everyone was encouraged to grow more food. Because less and less goods were able to be imported every household was compelled to save all kinds of waste.

Paper, cardboard and scrap metal, anything that could be re-used. It wasn't long before iron railings and gates were confiscated and sent to factories to be used for making armaments.

With air raids becoming more frequent the children who had been evacuated to the area were sent home again. Enemy planes began to fill the skies overhead, the sirens sounded more frequently and the ARP wardens were out patrolling the streets and fire watching. More Anderson shelters were built. These were made of corrugated iron laid over large trenches, which were then covered in sandbags. Some people put in beds and other furniture so that they could spend the whole night down there, if necessary. Morrison shelters were strong tables, made of metal and used indoors.

MEMORIES OF GEORGE WICKENS

The ashes from the paper mill were used to fill in the bomb craters at Eastchurch Aerodrome in the Second World War. I remember when bombs dropped on Dover Street, Park Road and Cockleshell Walk where all the houses were destroyed.

★ ★ ★

During raids over the town bombs fell on several streets in Sittingbourne and in Kemsley. Cockleshell Walk and Park Road were among those hit and people were killed. These raids continued into the following year and there was a fear of incendiary bombs. Fire watchers were trained to deal with these and both men and women were doing voluntary work as well as their regular jobs. Although voluntary in the sense that they were not paid, a certain number of hours were compulsory. Women were now employed in the mill and other factories as well as acting as telephonists for the ARP and the Fire Service. They also joined the Land Army, doing a valuable job helping to keep the nation fed. At first, the sight of women driving tractors and other machinery was not taken seriously but they soon proved their worth and earned a lot of respect; doing a difficult and sometimes dangerous job well.

MEMORIES OF RON SHEPHERD

During the war dad was in the ARP and we were never at home at night. My brothers were abroad in the army and we never knew when or if they were coming home so the front door was never locked. We couldn't lock the back door because the toilet was outside.

★ ★ ★

Other people did fire watching, spending nights on the roofs of factories and other buildings and the area was also protected by searchlight and anti aircraft units. One was at Tunstall and one at Chetney marshes.

MEMORIES OF DON KINGSNORTH

Blast walls, as they came to be called, were built, about 7 feet by eight feet; these were erected at the end of the alley ways between the blocks of terraced houses. On a piece of open ground, which is now called Millen Road, at the bottom of Charlotte Street, an air raid shelter was built of brick. I don't think it was ever used, most people seemed to think that it would be safer sitting outside than in.

The house we lived in during the war backed on to part of the mill that was unfinished and it was quite easy for us 'herberts' to climb on to the roof of the mill. As the war intensified the anti aircraft guns on Chetney Marshes and other local sites were letting fly at enemy planes, mainly at night, so there was always plenty of shrapnel to be found in the mornings. The roof of the mill was a good place to find it.

★ ★ ★

The local people were well aware that this war was being fought at home as well as at the front. The air raids were only a part of the battle. Everything was in short supply and in every home extra effort was made to save as much as possible and use as little as possible. Food was short and Dig for Victory became the watchword. Lawns and flower gardens were dug up and planted with vegetables; the need to save petrol and coal was urgent and everyone was asked to use less water as the pumping stations used coal. Kitchen waste was collected and fed to pigs and even such mundane items as rope and string had their uses.

Congregational Church where the British Restaurant was opened in 1942.

In 1942 a 'British Restaurant' was opened in the schoolroom of the Congregational Church in Crown Road and meals consisting of a dinner and a pudding could be bought there for less than a shilling. The air raids became less frequent but everyone was beginning to feel the pinch. By only heating one room, lagging pipes, blocking out drafts and putting bricks in the fire place, thereby using less coal, it was possible to survive, but life was grim during the winter of 1942/43. With no street lights and the buildings showing no lights, the streets were pitch black and the long winter evenings dragged on. With just one small fire in the house it was impossible to keep warm; even a soak in a hot bath was out of the question. No more than five inches of water was allowed.

Local people were not downhearted, though. Everyone helped each other and spirits remained high. Some public houses were closed but those that managed to stay open still drew the people in and although beer and spirits were, like everything else, in short supply a good old sing song did wonders for morale. Even though there was little enough to go round the local people still managed to collect food and extras to send to the troops. Fund raising was still going on, parties were being given for the children and many turned out to celebrate the Bank Holiday with a tea and sports day.

The relatively quiet time was ended at the beginning of 1944 when incendiary bombs were dropped on the town. Many houses were hit, as were several churches. Because the fire brigade was hard pressed to cope it was left to the people themselves to help put out fires and although they managed very well some shops and houses were badly damaged. This was also the year that saw the arrival of the V-1 flying bomb or the doodlebug as it was called. This type of warfare seemed to be very cold blooded, with no manpower needed it was sheer luck, or bad luck, where they fell.

One thing that happened to cheer everyone up was the arrival in the town of General Montgomery. He came to inspect the troops from in and around Sittingbourne and made a rousing speech which not only put new heart into the troops but also into the local people who went to watch. Later that year there was cause for celebration when news came through that Paris had been liberated. The bells of Milton's Holy Trinity Church rang out and several concerts were put on. Things started to be more relaxed as the blackout regulations became less severe and the Home Guard was disbanded.

Although there were still many restrictions in 1945 people began to realise that the end was in sight. Funds were still being raised, but not so much money was forthcoming, and the British Restaurant closed. It wasn't long before men who had been prisoners of war came home and the celebrations really began in earnest when Victory in Europe was announced. Church bells were rung, the lights went on again and services of thanksgiving were held all over the town. Street parties were held and even though food was still rationed and in short supply parents still managed to put on a good spread.

MEMORIES OF DON KINGSNORTH

The last part of the war was pretty uneventful for us children but when it was over it seemed as though there was a divide between the top and bottom halves of the street. The people at the top considered themselves better than us. This was made evident at street parties. The Foresters Arms pub is situated half way down the street and only the people who lived at the top end went to the street parties. Why this was so and why we at the other end never had a party I never knew but after that it was 'us and them'.

5. THE 1950s AND 60s

Even though rationing was to be with them for a few years after the war the people of Milton Regis hoped that life would become easier and more tranquil but early in 1947 the weather proved to be the enemy. Like the rest of the country the town was caught up in a great freeze and the area was one of the coldest, with 32 degrees of frost being recorded. There was a shortage of coal which not only caused great hardship in homes but also resulted in workers being put on short time.

More problems were to follow in January 1953 when the worst floods in living memory occurred. Strong winds and high tides had caused the sea wall to collapse and the Isle of Sheppey was cut off. In Milton Regis the land at Church Marshes was flooded, as were many houses and some people lost their homes.

MEMORIES OF MR & MRS CLARKE

We lived round the corner from Flushing Street. When we had the big flood on Saturday night Alice went down stairs and called out to me, 'I'm standing in water.'

At this time she was only half way down the stairs. I done no more and said to her, 'You can't be.'

I got up and put my slippers on, I don't know what for. To go into the scullery we had to go down two steps.

'We can't do nothing, I'll find some way of making a cup of tea,' as I said this the tide, which was still coming up, went straight over the top of the gas stove. It was frightening and we never did get our cup of tea. Our son was still upstairs in bed; his mum went back upstairs to tell him about the water. His reply was, 'Once it gets up to the bedroom window, I'll swim up the road.'

He just wouldn't get up.

The dog ran and got under the bedclothes with our lad. Our house was the first one to catch the tide because unbeknown to us there was a big hole in the alley where the force of the tide had lifted the cover off the drain from Bowater Mill. Up until the flood this had been covered by about eight feet of soil.

My brother lived Kingsmill Road, he was living on the edge of the creek and when the floods came I went out of the back door and had to swim all the way round. But before I reached his house, which was on the other side of the creek, I found I was on dry land. He lived right on the creek but didn't get flooded because the water had come our way.

★ ★ ★

Although 1953 saw what is generally referred to as the big flood, for the people who lived near the creek or the mill flooding was a part of their every day life.

MEMORIES OF ROY JARMAN

The down side of living on The Wall was that we often had floods, usually during the early hours of the morning, which meant that we had to move the furniture upstairs. I recall on one occasion getting stuck half way up the stairs with the settee, not being able to go up or down. To dry out our homes we would get coal from the mill. It was a regular trip to the gas works every morning before school to buy a couple of bags of coke. On returning home from school in the evening it was another trip to the gas works to collect more coke to keep other people's fires burning. We carried the bags on our shoulders and we used to sell it to various homes like public houses and others as far away as Unity Street. The money we earned from selling the coke meant that we could go to the cake shop, get a bag of bread for 3d, stale buns 2d or 3d and you would get quite a big bagful for that money.

MEMORIES OF DICKIE BISHOP

People who lived on The Wall had the outflow from the mill running under their houses and from time to time when the water rose our houses would be flooded. The furniture used to float. Sittingbourne Urban District Council would be quite generous and give each household a bottle of disinfectant and half a bag of coal to dry out their houses.

MEMORIES OF BOB WHITAKER

I was born in Mill Street, which was called the slum of Milton because it was next to the mill. At high tide the creek used to overflow and the water would come up the garden and flood our outside toilet.

MEMORIES OF RON SHEPHERD

The creek actually ran underneath our front room. It didn't smell in those days. Many of us children who lived in Milton learned to swim in Milton Creek. Where it used to come out of the mill the water used to be a different colour, depending on the colour of the paper that they were making. We liked to swim in this water because it was warmer than the fresh water. We didn't come out pink though! These days they pay to go swimming, we did it for free! When the tide came up, just the normal spring tides, the water came up to the windowsill.

Marshall Brunger used to pick us up at the 'Milton Arms' and bring us kids home from school in a boat.

* * *

Bowater's Mills continued to thrive; by this time there were more than 5,000 people working in them. The brickfields had closed for the duration of the war but when they re-opened the introduction of modern machinery meant less men were needed. Other factories opened in the area; Lowe's Dog Biscuit factory was joined, in 1950, by the Export Packing factory, these two firms backed on to the railway line.

Sittingbourne Shipbuilders became general freightage contractors and by the 50s many barges had been converted and motorised including the Hydrogen, Phoenician, Vicunia, Edith May and Trilby. They had also built auxiliary naval craft for the Second World War. These, of course, were not needed afterwards and as trade diminished the main buildings became warehouses.

The last barge sailed down Milton Creek in the 1950s, leaving only the motorised ones to do what little work was around and the dearth of traffic and the extraction of water by the mill caused the creek to silt up so much that it was only wide enough for one vessel. The lack of water and pollution from the mill caused a terrible smell to come from the creek in the summer time and there were complaints about it. At low tide it was said that it smelt like rotten eggs and eventually a campaign was successful in persuading the mill to do something about it.

The advent of television, in its early days, did nothing to spoil the people's fondness for going out to take part in club activities or to play or watch sport. Bowls, table tennis, swimming, cricket and darts all had their followers and Sittingbourne Football Club began to be successful, although some violence and money problems spoiled things a little. Smaller clubs were formed, encouraging younger people to play. Cinemas and pubs were still attracting customers and there was plenty of entertainment around catering for all tastes. One special event occurred in 1953 with the coronation of Queen Elizabeth II, which was marked by street parties, and other celebrations.

MEMORIES OF PETER MANTLE

In 1953 for the coronation of Queen Elizabeth II there were many street parties in Milton Regis. Backing on to our garden was Bennett Opie, the cherry factory and a fortnight before the coronation there was an eclipse of the sun. I spent hours in the shed at the bottom of our garden because I knew that as it was almost a total eclipse the girls were going to be let out of the factory to see it. They used wooden barrels in the factory which normally were laid on their bellies but on this occasion they stood them on their ends (the barrels, that is). One girl ran across to get a piece of smoked glass and jumped straight into a barrel, up to her waist in cherries.

Jesse May Mantle, Peter's mum cutting the cake at the party for the coronation of Queen Elizabeth II in Chalkwell Road

We used the land behind Bennett Opie for the celebration of the coronation and we prepared it for the occasion. There were presents and food for the children, of which I was one as I was ten years old at the time. There was a fancy dress contest, a girl named Barnes won; she was dressed as Elizabeth I. As Edmund Hillary had just conquered Mount Everest I was dressed like him and I wore a boiler suit, woollen hat, wellington boots and grey gloves and carried a rope and pick axe. The temperature was about 130 degrees Fahrenheit, or so it seemed to me in my boiler suit. I was screaming for a drink and someone said, 'You'll have to sit down at the table.'

I had to spend the whole of the party dressed like this and carrying a heavy rope I could hardly put one foot in front of the other. I felt like a baked potato, I got second prize. The lady who was destined to be my mother in law and her friend Ivy went as Laurel and Hardy.

★ ★ ★

At the beginning of the decade Milton Regis underwent even more changes. The North Court Housing Estate, which includes Saffron Way, Langley Road and Trinity Road, was built and the first houses were opened in 1953. Because there was no longer any danger of the creek overflowing houses could be built in this area which meant that for the first time in 900 years there were people living in the vicinity of Holy Trinity Church. Regis Crescent and Court Road were developed nearby on land that had once been home to brickfields.

The land surrounding the recreation ground was built on at this time and Dean Road, Laxton Way and other streets took the place of an orchard and rough scrubland where children used to play.

MEMORIES OF BETTY SETTERFIELD

I remember playing in what was called Knowles' orchard. One day I went out to play wearing my new red coat. We were messing about on this big, old log and I fell off. Unfortunately I landed in a large cow pat and got smothered. My mum was furious! She didn't even know that I had worn my new coat and I got into terrible trouble. After the war prefabs were built on the land where we used to play and later on they were taken down and streets of houses were built; Dean Road, Cherry Close and Laxton Way were some of them.

★ ★ ★

Over the next few years the town expanded in other directions with council houses going up in streets like Staplehurst Road. Private houses were also built there and in Beechwood Avenue and other streets. Land to the north of Vicarage Road had houses built on it and in 1958 a new school, Middletune Junior, was constructed and enlarged in 1962. The council spent money on renovating older properties and Court Hall was not forgotten.

Some time after it was completely restored it became a museum.

MEMORIES OF DON KINGSNORTH

It was during the 1960s that the orchards and fields of Milton started to disappear to be replaced by houses. An apple orchard, a lovely place to go scrumping, was between Charlotte Street and Chalkwell Road. Under the orchard was a stream, which surfaced in Church Street, ran for about sixty yards and disappeared underground again. This was the Periwinkle Stream which up until the 50s ran with clear water but then dried up because the water had been taken out by the mill.

★ ★ ★

With all the new houses being built it wasn't long before a decision was made to pull down the older properties, starting with the ones which had suffered much flooding. Houses in King Street, New Road, The Wall, Bridge Street and Flushing

Street disappeared and the occupants re-housed. Many of these were elderly and smaller homes and flats were built for them. However bad the conditions were that they had lived in for many years for some it was a wrench to leave and make a fresh start amongst new neighbours.

The demolishing of the streets also meant the end for many of the public houses that had played a large part in the lives of some of the local people. These establishments had been around for a very long time, with an occasional change of name being the only alteration to them. For example the 'Green Dragon' in King Street was originally 'The Dredging Smack'.

The Green Dragon, King Street.

Trinity Trading Estate was built in the 1960s behind the North Court Housing Estate. This land had also been brickfields owned by Wills and Packham. One of the firms on the estate is Milton Pipes, which was one of the last firms to have loads of sand and cement delivered via the creek.

There was a problem for the local council and for the residents when unauthorised caravan sites were set up by travellers. After being evicted from Sittingbourne they set up camp in Milton, first on Bowater's land and then at the Wall. Eventually they moved on to Church Marshes where they stayed for a number of years. Although most of the local people did not want the travellers in the town, over the years their language became incorporated into that of Milton's. Words such as cushty (good), wafty, (bad), chavvies (children) were heard in the pubs and streets. Wives and mothers were known as 'the old tiger' or 'the old mort' and if you heard someone enquiring after the 'old boy' they meant the son not the father.

6. MEMORIES OF GROWING UP

MARGIE HEARNDEN

Looking back over the years to my life in Milton Regis I think that I must have been a right little horror! I always seemed to be in trouble. Mr and Mrs Blackman had the dubious honour of me being born to them in Charlotte Street in 1911. There we all lived, my parents, two brothers and I. My brothers were called Tim and Les who later became the licensee of the 'Crown and Anchor' and the 'Harrow' at Stockbury and compared to me they were little gentlemen.

If there wasn't a fight going on I would start one and drag them both into it. One day one of my brothers went missing and we eventually found him swimming in the creek, stark naked. My mum was horrified! My brother, Tim, fancied himself as a violinist. Mum and dad managed to get him a violin and all day long 'Felix Kept on Walking'. One day I couldn't stand it any longer and I rubbed margarine all over the violin. That was the end of Felix, his walking days were over.

My dad used to often get drunk but he never got nasty with it, he was a real comic and as he approached the house he could be heard calling, 'I'm coming home, Ethel, I'm coming home!' My mum would say, 'I'll give him he's coming home' but she was very easy going and hardly ever had a go at him.

She never smoked or drank at all and her greatest pleasure was organising parties for other people and watching them enjoying themselves. His signature tune when drunk was 'Tiptoe Through the Tulips'. On one occasion we were expecting company who were a bit posh. Mum had told dad to be home in good time and when he didn't arrive we went to look for him. He was lying outside the pub so we managed to get him home and mum sat him in the armchair and draped a sheet over him. 'Don't you dare move', she said to him and when the company arrived she told them that we were decorating.

Many nights when he came home he had to sleep in the chicken run because he couldn't go any further. One night when he went out and got drunk he was wearing his new suit. He took it off when he came home and left it where the cat could get at it. That caused a lot of trouble because the cat had done its business on the suit. My dad shouted so loudly that the cat ran off, never to be seen again. Luck would have it that he was sober the day that my friend and I quarrelled over a chicken. He chopped off the head and feet gave these to my friend and we had the rest.

The bread and milk were delivered to the house by horse and cart, the horse usually leaving his calling card by the door. This was always good for a few swear words. The biggest mistake of my youth was trying to ride a bicycle; I fell off many times and once I fell into a hole which the workmen had dug at the end of the street. That bicycle ended its days nailed to my bedroom wall.

ALICE CLARKE

When I was at school I had a friend whose father was a lighter man and I used to go with her on the lighters from the creek to Ridham Dock and come back on the bogies. We used to make our own fun with things like skipping ropes and spinning tops.

ERNEST CLARKE

There was always a lot going on in Milton, we used to go round the creek, swimming and underneath us was the foam from the mill, we used to sit in the drain amongst all the sludge, yet we were never ill, we used to love it! It seemed to me that anyone who never swam in the creek was constantly ill. Redshaws, the cockle people, they used to go out fishing and sell the stuff they caught. They had a fish and chip shop in the New Road where they sold the fish that they caught.

When you go round that way now you would not believe how many people lived in that small space. It has seen some changes over the years; goodness knows how many pubs there were. The Lion in Mill Street is a house now. On the other side of the road was a stone masons, where they made headstones for graves, Millens, (it could be that the ones removed from the churchyard in Crown Road in February 1998 were made here).

ROY JARMAN

I was born in the nineteen twenties at number 1 Eastbourne Street, Sittingbourne where I lived with my grandmother. We moved to The Wall in Milton Regis when I was five. I had two brothers and one sister, but my sister died of cancer when she was twenty. Everyone we knew was poor and we used to run around with no shoes on. We often went to the cake shop where we could buy a bag of bread for 3d and stale buns for 2d or 3d and for that you would get quite a big bag full. Visits to the shops in Sittingbourne were not very frequent as we could find everything we needed in Milton.

In those days we used to go to the Salvation Hall which had seats all the way round. There was usually music being played and we were given tea and biscuits. That was a regular thing to do every weekend. Right near there was Buggs's food shop on the corner of Mill Street and about fifteen to twenty children used to go there. We played skipping in Short Street as there was hardly any traffic around in those days. Bowater's clubhouse, where there was a bandstand was another place where we could go to listen to music and have a cup of tea as well.

Another place that we enjoyed playing in was the brickfield. We would pull a brick out of one of the stacks and then run round and upset the gatekeeper. He used to chase us round the stacks and on one occasion he knocked one of the bricks out of a stack and the whole lot fell on top of him.

I fell through the ice one Christmas and someone from the corner shop came and pulled me out, it was on a Sunday and I was dressed in my best clothes. Mum was not at all pleased! I also fell in a pug hole once; a pug hole was where they poured liquid to make the pug from which bricks were made.

One of our prize possessions was a gramophone but it didn't have a needle so we used the head of a pin and we became very popular by playing the same old record over and over again.

BOB WHITAKER

In Mill Street, where we lived, I remember my mother used to say, 'We may be poor but the people next door are even poorer.'

On the floor in our house we had rag rugs but the next door neighbours only had coal sacks.

One memory I have of my father is of him saying to my mother, 'Bertha, give us a latch lifter.'

The Lion pub in our street had a latch instead of a door handle so the saying was: will you let me have the money for a latch lifter, about 6d, to get in pub. For that amount you could stay drinking in the pub, till chucking out time. This was in the early thirties. He was a barge captain, as was my grandfather and great grandfather. They were Shrubsalls, a very well known family locally.

When I was five, in 1932, we moved to Charlotte Street; my grandparents lived just below us. I remember my great grandparents very well. He was a short dumpy man and she always wore her hair in a bun. Great granddad died and she sat by his coffin for about two days without moving, until she died too. She died of a broken heart. They were buried together in Milton churchyard; you can still see the stone. They had ten children, my grandmother Charlotte was called Lottie. One brother Reuben was killed in 1915, in the First World War, I am named after him, but my family always called me 'bruv' because when I was in my pram my brother Fred, who was two years older than me, used to say 'That's my bruvver.'

I went to live with my gran when the Second World War started. Lottie Smith her name was and she was stone deaf. Her husband died of consumption (TB). I lived with gran all through the war. We didn't have television or radio, I would sit doing my homework and gran would say, 'Let me do the writing, cause I'm better at writing than you' - and she was. She would often tell me about the days when she was a little girl, when the landed gentry and their ladies used to come down to the elite part of Milton in their carriages and four.

She left school at a very early age, and often told me about her days when she was in service. Parents couldn't afford to keep their children so they had to go out to work. My mother

Salvation Army Hall in Bridge Street.

was in service in London and she hated it so she saved her pennies until she had enough money to run away. She caught a train to Newington, because that's as far as the train went. She got off and there were some soldiers on the platform and they asked her where she was going. She told them 'Sittingbourne' so one of them asked her if she would like to walk with them and she did. That soldier remained a friend until the day she died.

Mill Street was where Tommy Buggs had his shop, opposite the Salvation Army hall. He was known as Lord Mayor of Milton. My mother belonged to the Salvation Army. In Milton High Street there was a shoe shop where we used to pay 2s 6d a week to pay for the family's shoes. Then there was Mellows the dentist, a pub with green tiles, a rag and bone man and just round the corner was Mr Lights the hairdresser who used to cut my hair. Children enjoyed themselves by making their own fun. I remember when we had a relay put in for the wireless for 1s.9d a week we were considered 'posh'.

Before I left Borden Grammar School in 1943 I tried to get a Saturday job but with no success, not even a paper round! I used to do my great aunt's shopping. Her name was Heason and she lived in William Street. Even though there was a Co-op in Park Road she insisted that I went all the way to the one at East Street to do her shopping. I got tuppence for doing that. That Co-op was near the Plaza cinema but all those buildings are gone. There's a doctor's surgery there now.

MRS F KEEL

I was born in 1929, in Cross Lane which is behind Court Hall. Soon afterwards we moved to Albion Cottages, behind the almshouses in the Butts. I went to the school there and I remember the big house, called Langley House which was an orphanage for boys. The girls were housed in Green Porch, next to the church. I can remember the boys marching to and from the school and they had to go every day to the workhouse to do the gardening. I used to watch them come back up North Street, round Brewery Road and go into the house. When the war started they were moved away and Langley House became part of the school.

It was very pleasant living round there in those days. There were brickfields, the rope walk, which was a very long, red tin building and of course the light railway going to and fro but there were also orchards, allotments and fields where we could play.

Almshouses at the Butts

GEORGE WICKENS

I enjoyed my life in Milton when I was young. The day the circus came to town watching the elephants being watered at the Periwinkle Stream was great fun. Billy Seagar once jumped off the bridge into Milton Creek for a tuppeny bet; we all thought this was a very clever thing to do at the time but of course now I realise it was quite dangerous. At the weekend we often used to play in the brickfield and make camps, using the bricks that were lying about, and we also slid down the banks on an old sledge that we made.

There was a large yard at The Wall where a man called Mr Mane stored the wood that he used to make caravans for the gypsies. These caravans were very flashy we were really impressed by them. I used to watch the Baker family work; they sold horses and would trot them up and down the street so people could see what they were like before they bought them.

When we were kids we all had jobs to do before we were allowed out to play. My job was to fetch a bag of coke from the ashes at Lloyd's Paper Mill to help keep the open fire going.

In the summer we would swim in the creek and watch the barges sailing in to unload their cargoes of clay, coal and wood pulp for the paper mill. In the New Road was a barber's shop owned by Gus Cannon who charged 3d for a haircut. He had an assistant who he called 'shaver' and he would send the boy into the 'Lion' public house two or three times a day to buy him a jug of beer. None of us boys liked having our hair cut at the end of the day because his hands were shaking by then.

In those days local pubs were always packed. The most popular one was the 'Watermans Arms' and often sailors would stop us in the street and ask the way to it. On Sundays we had a special treat for tea of cockles and whelks from Mrs Redshaw's fish shop in the New Road, there was usually live flat fish on a plate in the window. Local character Marshal Brunger would sometimes come to our house to sell us six flat fish on a string for which he charged half a crown and we would have these for tea. One of Marshal's sayings was 'All you need is your health, if you've got that you can always go out and earn a bob or two.'

DICKIE BISHOP

My mates and I could only have been about ten years old when we used to go down to the closed down brickfield with our dog and chase the rabbits out of the hole. This brickfield was in Cook's Lane where there are now private houses.

Summer used to seem longer in those days, we went fishing in a pond in Gas Lane, it was great! We had a few frights, getting caught when we pinched coal and coke from Percy Payne, the coal merchant, and the local gas works. Two of us would go over the wall and pass bags full of the stuff to the lads on the other side. After having our ears clipped lots of times we gave this lark up. Of all the games we used to play I remember most the catapult and bow and arrow fights. These were quite painful and one poor boy even lost an eye during one of these games.

In 1955, with my pals Lenny and Tony, I was digging for brick earth in Quinton fields when we uncovered what looked like a coffin. We got the lid off but there was nothing inside. One of my mates said that it looked as though it was made of lead. So we took it to the local scrap merchant who bought it from us for £2. We thought we were very rich. Every winter Cornford's lake would freeze over so we would all go skating, it's a wonder we never broke our necks.

Placed around the Mill Street area were several public houses, namely: 'The Waterman's Arms', 'The Crown and Anchor', 'The Green Dragon' and 'The King's Arms'. We were often entertained by fights taking place outside these pubs and especially outside 'The Waterman's Arms' every Saturday night. There were quite a few well known local characters who played the piano in these pubs and the regulars enjoyed a good sing song. Three I remember in particular were Sid Smith, Tiny Spence and Tich May. They always put on a good show.

When I was fourteen years old I started work in the brickfield at Church Marshes for £2.19s a week. For this sum we worked a sixty-six hour week. One of the best sights around, for me, was the barges coming into Milton Creek to be unloaded at the Milton Brick and Cement Works. There was the Charles Burley, the Scud and the Ninety Nine, the latter broke its back on the mud and had to be towed off by a tug. For three days they tried to re-float it and failed.

One day I was out poaching with a mate when the farmer appeared on the scene, so what did we do? We tied him to the tree and carried on poaching. The poor chap wasn't found till much later that day. Oops!!

DON KINGSNORTH

I was born in December 1931 at 9 Frederick Street although we moved from there long before I was old enough to know any one. I did move back within stomping distance when I was older and it is now firmly etched on my mind. This is mainly because of the corner shop there, owned by Freddy Mockett, a true gentleman.

One of my earliest memories is of living in a large house in Milton High Street and a story told to me by my father, who I am proud to say, won a military medal in the First World War. The tale concerned a policeman who called at the house one day who, when the door was opened, placed his foot on the doorstep. Our large alsatian dog put his head between my father's legs and grabbed hold of the policeman's trouser leg. He didn't make any fuss, saying to my father that he was to blame as he shouldn't have put his foot there.

Our next move was to a house in Church Street where the view from the front room window was of a brick wall, thirty feet high, belonging to Bowater's mill. From there we moved to the bottom end of Charlotte Street. Between the 'Forester's Arms' and the rest of the houses there was a piece of land that occasionally became a battleground. The louts from the bottom half of the street would have a brick and stone throwing battle with some of the tearaways from the Frederick Street area. Although there were never any outright winners of these battles I have, to this day, scars over my eyes which prove that I couldn't duck fast enough.

Sometimes, after we finished school for the day and had our tea we would go to the Rec where there was a row of very large pear trees running through the middle. When the fruit was ready for picking we would throw bricks up into the trees and knock them down. Once I threw up a brick and, bending down for another, I looked up and my head met the first one coming down. As a result of this I had two stitches and another scar to my collection.

Also at the Rec were swings, seesaws and a maypole and a building which was the pavilion, although we called it a many sided summerhouse. This was built of brick with the top half made of wood and glass and there were wooden benches inside.

We used to play in it although I think it was meant for the grownups to sit in. It remained in good condition throughout our childhood and when we started work it was a popular place for courting.

I'll never forget some of the meals my mum cooked for us. On Sundays she would make a big plain suet pudding. She used to cut it in half and we would have a piece with our roast dinner and a piece for afters with jam on. My favourite, though, was steak and kidney pudding which she used to wrap in a muslin cloth and boil on the top of the stove in a huge saucepan. When it was cooked she would unwrap it, cut into the suet crust and pour the gravy on to the meat. Delicious! Another dinner I remember is smoked haddock, you could smell it long before you reached home.

Like other children in the area I paid regular visits to the local gas works to buy coke. Sometimes I had to queue but I always got a barrow load. Any money my friends and I had was spent in the local sweet shop owned by Mr Spall. It was half way down Milton Hill and very old fashioned. We had our hair cut by a barber called Jimmy Stevens who had one leg shorter than the other. He wore a special boot on the short leg but unfortunately it was not completely successful as it did not make his legs the same length. As he cut our hair the clippers went up and down to the rhythm of his limp which meant that our hair ended up looking like a staircase. We always went to him, though, because he was a nice old man and he always chatted to us.

Round about the end of the war I passed the exam to go to Sheerness Technical School, now regretfully no longer in existence, and we used to travel to school by train. These journeys were livened up by the Italians in a prisoner of war camp on Queenborough marshes. There were some good artists at the camp and all the doors were very colourful with lively pictures. The prisoners used to wave to us as we passed them.

RON SHEPHERD

At the top end of the Wall the numbers went from 5 to 10 and that part was actually in Sittingbourne. I was born on January 3rd 1934 at number 5 The Wall and then later we moved to number 5a The Wall which is in Milton. The reason we moved was because we needed an extra bedroom as our family consisted of 6 girls and 4 boys. I went to Holy Trinity School in Dover Street, which is still in use as a school. Because it was a church school we had to go to church at Christmas and Easter and the church was very cold in those days. There was no heating like today, all they had was a pot bellied fire at one end, where the vicar stood, and that was all.

A regular thing in those days to raise money was to pawn things, a favourite one being dad's suit, in the pawnshop Monday - out Friday ready for a visit to the pub. Our family didn't do any pawning because as there were so many of us mum used to sell sweet coupons to people who had more money than us; she also sold some clothing coupons so we had to make our clothes last longer and then we had money for other things.

My mum used to go fruit picking and when she went hop picking we all went with her. When we were very small we went up to Woodstock, to the hopping huts, which were just bare huts with straw where we slept for six weeks, all in the same room. We used to cook outside on a stove under a lean-to.

We would climb over the wall of the mill and go on to the ashes where they kept the waste paper print and comics. We never had to buy any comics or anything like that. Whilst sorting through the waste paper we often got chased off.

My father worked at Kemsley Mill. We had everything we wanted in Milton. There was Milton Rec where we used to play. We never had pocket money, if you wanted an apple from the shop we bought specked ones, because they were cheaper than the good ones.

Milton Rec had a row of pear trees, which have since been chopped down; we used to go scrumping. These belonged to the council but they couldn't watch us all the time so we got away with it quite often. My friends Eddie Glass and Peter Cannon, who lived in the same road as Bobby Carroll, their fathers all worked either in the mill or on the barges. I also remember the Cornelius family, they and the Wellards and Baileys lived in the same road, at the bottom of Milton Hill. The actual road, or part of it, is still there.

We moved from The Wall and moved up to what is known as Anne's Cottage. This was a big house next to the Ivy Leaf Club with billboards alongside. Opposite there is a railway bridge made of metal and the trains made a terrible noise. Once we got used to it we never noticed it until one night the trains didn't run and we couldn't sleep and we wondered what was keeping us awake. It was the silence!

For our holidays we used to go to Sheerness once a year and when we went there we had ice creams. We went to Margate a couple of times, with the Ivy Leaf, which was the British Legion, because my father was a member. We had to wear a tag with our name and address on.

It was usual for children to wear hand-me-downs and short trousers but I was lucky, being seventeen years younger than my elder brother, all my clothes were new. I left school at 14 and went to work for six months to pay for my first pair of long trousers, so I was fourteen and a half before I wore long ones; small boys didn't wear such things in those days. Today the children wear long trousers as soon as they start school. At least we didn't wear out the knees.

I used to like walking, with my friends I would walk from Norton over the King's Ferry Bridge round to Windmill Creek. We used to do a lot of shooting, rabbits and ducks. Every Saturday night my father would re-stud our boots; he would replace the ones that were worn out, after a time they would look like armour plating, the boots were also hand-me-downs. Because us kids used to go out for the whole day on Saturdays and Sundays, we never came home for dinner or tea, as I went out of the door mum would always call out,' Don't you dare come home here dead!'

The only places of entertainment were clubs and pubs in Milton so we went to a cinema in Sittingbourne. The Plaza was the cheapest so we usually went there. This was in East Street opposite the Co-op. It had just one storey, no balcony, and when you went through the doors you turned right or left, up the raked (sloping) floor and the screen was behind you. If you sat in the back row and dropped anything you could hear it roll all the way down to the front. So when you did you waited till it stopped and then went and picked it up. We used to go to the Saturday matinees and see such films as 'Flash Gordon'; everybody would pay on Saturday as we knew we were being watched. During the week, just one of us would pay and then let all the others in through the back door. We would pool our money for the one who had to pay. He would open the doors in the toilet so that the rest of us could get in. We would enter the cinema one at a time so as not to look suspicious. The Odeon was the easiest one to get into. The side door was in Bell Lane; there were three cinemas: the Odeon, the Plaza and the Queens. The attendants there used to come round in the interval and spray the cinema to get rid of the fleas.

VALERIE HEARNDEN

Looking back now, I realise that the houses in Bridge Street were not very nice. There were five houses but only four toilets between them, the old bench type with a hole in the middle, and we all shared the same backyard.

My thoughts very often go back to the days of my youth in Milton and I remember the lovely people

Shop belonging to Cllr Tommy Buggs in Mill Street.

who lived there. Following on from Bridge Street was Mill Street which was all cobble stones. There was a general store there, which was owned by Tommy Buggs who was also a local councillor. Opposite was Flushing Street where Mrs Higgins had a sweet shop and she also ran the local Brownie group. We spent a lot of time gazing in her shop window at all the jars and boxes of lovely goodies which made our mouths water. Mrs Shrubsall ran a fruit and vegetable cum sweet shop. She always let her customers pay at the end of the week; this was known as putting it on the book.

In St Paul's Street was Mrs Porter's sweet and vegetable shop, she was a sweet little old lady with white hair and glasses and she used to let me help her weigh the potatoes, which I thought was great. The shop owned by Mr Thames was a very interesting one. It was a curious mixture, with one half being a shoeshop and the other half a pot menders. Here people brought their saucepans to be repaired and they could buy mantles for their gas lamps. In Kingsmill Road lived Jimmy the barber where we all, boys and girls, had our hair cut. He was also the local bookmaker. I remember on one particular occasion the road was flooded but Jimmy was not going to be done out of his pint so he rowed himself across the road in a canoe to the 'Green Dragon'. The landlady there was known as Aunt Mabel, she not only ran the pub but did dressmaking as well. Many a local wedding party was dressed by her. Where did she find the time?

Times were hard those days but most people were cheerful and willing to help each other. I will always be grateful to my dear mum and dad who worked so hard yet got so little in return. Dad worked for the local council and mum used to go hop picking and did other field work so as to have enough money to clothe us. They also managed to give us a shilling which was enough to take us either to the pictures or the swimming baths on a Saturday morning. Yes, times were hard but I don't remember ever being unhappy.

PETER MANTLE

I was born in Chalkwell Road in Milton and lived there until I got married at the age of 21. My dad was an engine driver on the Bowater's line, doing shift work and his run was between Sittingbourne and Ridham Dock. My mum was a cleaner at Bennett Opie, the cherry factory. The first thing my dad liked when he finished his shift was a pint, even better if he had one in the wood at the 'Grapes' pub. The Grapes was where the roundabout now is, at the bottom of Chalkwell Road where it meets Crown Road. That was their local. If he was working a twelve hour shift mum and dad would pop out for a pint and I would be left to my own devices. I usually went up the Rec. There was a street light there and me and my mates would be footballers, playing for England. This was during the fifties and about this time floodlights were being introduced and the continental football kits were as well.

One Christmas time I had a big disappointment because my mum and dad, with the best intentions, bought me a football kit in Sittingbourne colours, red and black, with football boots to complete the outfit. They must have worked their fingers to the bone to get them for me. It was at this time that Sittingbourne changed their kit to the continental 'V' neck but mine had a collar and long sleeves. I thought I would get away with cutting off the collar and sleeves with a pair of scissors but it went all jagged. And did I get into trouble for that! Not that my mates had the new ones either! These days changing strips is a regular occurrence. It only happened every ten years when I was young; I got the tenth year! I was upset by all this and I thought 'next year I'll have a train set. Mum and dad said, 'You won't be able to have a train set, we won't be able to afford it.' The next Christmas arrived and lo and behold so did the train set. It was an underground train so it never had an engine. There I was with three carriages that went both ways. I was heartbroken! Fancy having a train set without an engine. I have been to a lot of toy fairs since then and I have never seen an underground train set. If I had kept that set it might have been worth a few bob now.

When I was little I had to go shopping for my mum and some of the shops used to open on Sunday evenings. There was one particular shop, right down by the creek, I had been sent down there with a shopping bag and a list. I'm not sure if the barges were still running, I think there may have been a few, and the men from the barges used to stay in the lodging houses opposite the shop. I'm standing by the shop counter with my list waiting to be served when a woman came flying out of one of the lodging houses, like a bat out of hell, came into the shop and grabbed me from behind and threw me to the ground.

She shouted, 'Don't you ever cross my path again, Billy Mane.'

I was so scared I started crying, saying I'm not him but she'd gone by then and from the road she called, 'Don't you ever forget that lesson, Billy Mane.'

I was not a pal of Billy Mane, we never played together although I knew him, he came from the heart of Milton.

The next time our paths crossed was when the place where I worked wanted a piece of metal cut and someone said it might be a good idea to go to the engineering factory down the road.

'They have a big machine that will cut that for you,' I was told.

I phoned the firm and they said they would be happy to help and I was told to go there and ask for Mr Mane. On my arrival a bloke called out, 'Someone for you Bill, a Mr Mantle.'

He came out and said, 'Mantle? You're Peter Mantle.'

'And you're Billy Mane,' I replied.

They cut the metal for me and I was about to leave and he said, ' Hey Peter that's one you owe me.'

And I said, 'No Bill, I think we're even.'

His reply was, 'You blokes up your way could never add up.'

I thought, no! We met up again some time later and I told him the story and his reply was that the clout from the woman could have been for lots of reasons.

They were not bad times to grow up in, on the whole. You were safe walking about outside but if you did anything wrong you got a clip round the ear from grownups. I was a paperboy and worked for Peter Birch. We had to collect the money from customers on Saturday mornings and for this I got £2 a week. I must have had the biggest round in Milton. I used a bike to do the paper round, like they do now, except on Saturdays when I wanted to get done quickly so we could go to the pictures. Our favourite treat to take to the pictures was a French loaf that we bought from Barrows the Bakers. We ate this inside and kept the crusts to throw to the birds when we came out.

Collecting money off the customers, I would knock on the door, and I had twenty to thirty houses on Milton Hill, and if I got the money from a couple of them I did well. I knocked on the door and they shouted, 'Come in,' I would go in the front room and they would say, 'You ain't come for that money, 'ave you?' and they would be lying in bed. I'd say, 'Yes,' and a voice from the bedroom would cry out, 'Well you ain't getting none, anyway the paper you delivered on Tuesday was torn and I'm gonna see old Birchy about you.'

At the junction of Crown Road and Milton Hill there used to be a cafe which was owned by my godmother and her husband and they cooked good meals and let rooms to drivers overnight. Occasionally, on a Saturday morning, when I wasn't doing my paper round I would go and see my Aunt Flo. She always called me Pete Boy. She would say, "Pete Boy, you've got to have a cup of tea." The cafe was always busy and on a table in front of him, Ern, her husband would have a big bowl of butter and loads of bread, which was nice and thick 'cause they sliced their own. He would put the butter on the bread and it would be passed to me to scrape it off from round the edges. I'd do half a dozen of these and walk behind him, scraping the butter from the knife back into the dish.

Everyone one would have a normal lunch hour except for Mr Chesson, the barber, because he worked through. His was delivered to him and he would eat it between haircuts. After lunch I would slip over and collect the plates and he would pay up at the end of the week.

During the summer holidays my aunt used to have underprivileged children down from London. The bill was met by the London Authorities. She had them from four to six weeks. They mainly came down by train and she was so popular that the same youngsters came each year. They were called Omah, Hassan, Reg and Bill. She sent them round to my house and we would go off on great adventures and get home at teatime.

I know memories can be deceptive but I can never remember it raining. I always had a football and when I first met the boys I wrote on the football, in great big letters, this football belongs to...... One morning, off we went down Hythe Road with the football under my arm, the England team ready to beat anyone. The ball went straight through somebody's bay window in Hythe Road. We hid but no one came out so one of the lads said that the best thing to do was to run for it. We were out all day and when I got home and the lads had gone back to the cafe I had my tea and stayed in all evening. Father was sitting in his chair holding the football with my name on it. I couldn't get out of it so I said I didn't kick it. It ended up with my dad paying for the window.

Milton Athletic Football Club was in existence when I was young so it must have been going for over fifty years. They are still playing. If you didn't have any money you could watch them play at Milton Rec but if you wanted to watch Sittingbourne play at the Bull ground you had to wait until half time and then you could get in there for nothing. The characters of Milton played for Athletic, it was a very good team and they played in blue tops and white shorts. They always went round with a collecting box at the ground.

At this time there were street traders and the wet fish man came around and he'd cry out, "Alive, all alive!" There were tradesmen with barrows and rag and bone men. Me and my mate would collect jam jars from people's houses and take them up to Knight's yard to get money for them. At the top of Hythe Road was a renegade rag and bone man who came with his horse and cart. Although he was on someone else's territory no one ever challenged him and he knocked on doors collecting tin baths and all sorts. One day he was coming down the road, where there was a bit of an incline, and somebody spooked his horse which made it bolt, dragging the cart behind it. The rag and bone man was nowhere to be seen. The horse went straight across Chalkwell Road, over our low wall and straight through our front room window. The horse was in the front room, which was our best room, and the cart was in the garden. I don't remember how we got the horse out or whether it was hurt.

One weekend my dad had been out for his usual pint at the 'Grapes' and when he came home he had a goat with him. It was a billy goat with tiny horns, he was a loveable little thing. I don't know where he got it from but he put it in the chicken run. It seemed content at first but after a week or two he got fed up with the chicken run and started butting people.

My Aunt Lil lived on one side of the road and my other aunt lived opposite. It was normal in those days for families to live close to each other. We decided to put a running wire in the garden and put the goat on a dog's lead. The wall that the wire was fixed to was about four or five feet high and it wasn't long before the goat realised that my aunt next door kept chickens. He regularly leapt over the wall, and he was growing bigger all the time and he would fall over the other side, this is as far as he could travel. He couldn't get near the chickens but he had a good try. He was found most days hanging over the garden wall. It was about this time that it was decided that he had to go because apart from the chicken side of the garden he used to go next door to the other side, who were keen gardeners. They had a lovely selection of vegetables and that was all the signal he needed to have a feast.

In Milton there was a place called the Meads, which was a short cut through the Gore Court cricket ground. There was a fellow there who had all sorts of animals so dad decided to take the goat to him. My mum and I were looking out of the front bedroom window, which overlooked Hythe Road, we were both crying our eyes out as my dad led Billy up the road on a lead. Mum said, 'He's grown, he's a big goat now and he's gone to be with the other big goats to have a good time.'

I didn't realise until much later that he'd gone to be put down.

We had a dog called Trix, and it didn't matter what we did to keep her in she always managed to escape. There were complaints from people, far and wide. She loved to go in their goldfish ponds. Trix had two litters of puppies, fifteen in all; my father found good homes for them all.

Once when my mum and dad went out my friends and I decided to play sailors. The only thing we could find resembling a boat was the tin bath that hung on the wall in the garden, next to the food safe. There were so many of us crammed into our boat on rough seas that we managed somehow to split the back of the bath. When we got out the split, which was about three or four inches long, didn't show. I thought, well we don't put much water in the bath it won't reach that high and won't leak. However, my mum was the next person to use it, while I waited in the kitchen for my turn, and suddenly we heard her screaming. She had leaned back in the bath and the crack had opened and closed, pinching her skin in the process. The more she pulled forward the more it gripped her. Dad managed to release her and put dettol on the wound and he then turned to me and said, 'You know something about this, don't you?'

Near Kemsley Mill there's a place called Castle Rough (Alfred the Great) and round the back there were some Christmas trees and I went on a lone mission to get one. I dug it up and dragged it home and dad said, 'You've stolen that, haven't you? It's not yours to dig up! The place where you got it from is private property. Someone grows them for a living. You can take it back and replant it.'

I was in a very bad mood and I was half a mile from Castle Rough when I saw some men coming up the path. I thought, 'If they see me I'll go to prison.' I jumped on top of a potato van and laid flat and when they had gone I slipped off the top, hanging by my thumb. It broke! After I had spent all day doing what I thought was a nice surprise, all I ended up with was a broken thumb.

MORRIS LEWRY

There were many memorable characters living in Milton when I was a child. There was Emma who lived at The Wall and she was very friendly with the men. She was known as Long Emma because of her shape. She was a very tall lady with an extremely long neck around which she always draped a tight silk scarf. It was rumoured that at some time or other she had had her throat cut but we never found out if it was true. Her language was somewhat blue and anyone who upset her, knew it! She was, however, a very kindly lady and if anyone was in trouble she would be the first to help.

Another character was Bill King. He loved football and he supported Sittingbourne and he was there for practically every home game. He never knew who the opponents were but it didn't matter to him, whoever they were he would always call out, "Come along, Chatham." He liked to run round the ground upsetting other supporters.

Mabel Batchelor had a shop in Staplehurst Road which still stands. It was a small general shop of which there were many in those days. I can picture her as a little old lady; we used to go in there on the way to school. Jim Stevens was a barber and his little shop was opposite the 'Green Dragon' and this pub was notorious and quite often on our way home, late, we'd go by it and find people being thrown out but never saw any invited in. His shop used to fascinate us no end. Like many barbers in those days he used to take bets on the horses from customers.

The Mane family lived in a caravan on The Wall opposite the ash dump. This was by a stream that was hot because it came from the paper mill and as the heat rose it warmed the caravan. We used to go round and see old Mrs Mane; we all reckoned she was two hundred years old as she was like a walnut. Every time we saw her she seemed to age another hundred years.

7. MEMORIES OF WORK AND PASTIMES

ALICE CLARKE

When we grew older the only fun I ever had was when I was courting Ernie. We used to go to Sheppey a lot and to Ramsgate. We often went to the pictures and he would buy me a bar of brazil nut chocolate. Dancing was a regular pastime; we would meet at Sittingbourne Town Hall, as there weren't any dances in Milton. The only places of entertainment in Milton were pubs so unless you liked a drink you had to go to Sittingbourne.

ERNEST CLARKE

When I was on the dole, with £1 6s a week, my sister's husband, who was a great mate, used to treat me to a trip to the pictures when I had no money. He worked in the mill. I and my mates, Buster and Jimmy West, used to cycle to Sheerness and when we got to the clock we would turn into the Broadway and go into the cafe there. There was a garden at the back where we used to sit and eat cream cakes and all that. On one occasion when we had finished eating we discovered that none of us had any money so I said, 'I'll go outside and see if I can find someone we know from Sittingbourne to borrow some money from them.'

I was all right, I was out, wasn't I! And what do you think? Who should come along but my brother and it must have been the worried expression on my face that made him say to me, 'What do you want?'

I said, 'Buster and Jimmy can't get out of the cafe because we haven't paid for our tea.'

'How much do you want,' he asked?

I said, 'Only half a crown.'

So he lent me the money and I went back in and paid the bill. So he saved the day for us. Mind you I had already got out and I could have left those two there.

I played football for Sheppey, my brother Charlie was Captain of the team, and amongst the other players was Bert Lightening. In the local paper, sometime in 1997, was a photograph of an old Sheppey Team and the paper wished to know if any reader could name them and in particular who hit the Sheppey man on the head with a bottle. We knew who it was, we saw it happen, but never said anything. I also played football for Canning Town Glass Works. This happened because when I was out of work my brother said, 'Why not go over to the bottle works at Queenborough you might get a job there.'

I went to see the gaffer who said that as I played football for Whistable if I was to transfer to Canning Town football team I could have a job. So that's how I came to work there. My brother Charlie worked there all his life, he lived in Murston. He used to cycle home after work, get changed and cycle back to Sheerness because he was courting Nancy Budd.

When I first met my wife her mum and dad were always rowing. It didn't matter how tall or short you were you had to be able to catch because every time you walked into the room a plate would come flying at you. They were always fighting and it would end up with all four of us getting stuck in.

RON SHEPHERD

When I was sixteen there were quite a few dance halls in Sittingbourne. There was the new Drill Hall in Crown Quay Lane where they held dances once a week and Sittingbourne Club House had dances every Monday night and it cost 1 shilling to go in. The old drill hall is up East Street near the Plaza. It looks a bit like a church. It cost 6d to go in the cinema, 1 shilling to go in the dance halls except Carmel Hall in Ufton Lane which was only 9d. This one was a church hall so it didn't have a bar, they only sold soft drinks. I started off by working in the brickfields and after that I went to Brown Bros. as a lorry driver's mate. From there I went into the mill before I was called up to do two years National Service. I was in the Royal Artillery and they asked us where we wanted to be posted,

Malta, Gibraltar or Germany. We all said we didn't want to go to Germany so we were all sent there. I spent twenty months out there. After I came out of the army I spent two years working for a firm that makes breeze blocks in Crown Quay Lane and then I worked in Kemsley Mill. I was there for 41 years.

I first met my wife while I was in the army, when I was twenty. We got married in 1955 and lived at Kemsley with my in-laws. We then went to live at the back of Gore Court; it was a big house and an old lady lived there. We lived in the servants quarters which consisted of seven rooms. We stayed there for about two years and then we were allocated a house near the mill because I worked there.

One of the local characters was Dickie Bishop. He was known for being a poacher. Later in life he was unlucky when a nail went through his boot and caused gangrene in his legs. Subsequently he had to lose both legs but he was still a great character. Milky Bill was another poacher; he lived opposite Milton School and always had a ferret in his pocket. We never had to lock our front doors until the 1960s.

BOB WHITAKER

One day when I arrived home my mum told me that Jim Bedelle had called, he was a friend of mine at school. His father was Mr Bedelle, the newsagent and he was, for a long time, the chairman of the local council. His shop was right at the bottom of Park Road; I went down to see him and he said that there was a job going on the farm where he worked for 6d an hour. I went off with him the next day to Great Grovehurst Farm at Iwade. The first week was spent picking up dropped apples and putting them in bushel boxes. There were a lot of boys working there. I remember working down there from 1940 to 1942 during the summer and autumn holidays. The winter holidays were spent down the Co-op Dairies in East Street, working from 5.30am washing bottles.

The first five weeks I worked on the farm earned me £5 and I went down to Regoes, the clothing shop in Sittingbourne

High Street and bought myself an Alan Ladd mac which was a trench coat. Five pounds was a lot of money in those days but I had that mac for years. The chap in charge of us on the farm was Roy Andrews and when I left school in 1943 he asked me if I was coming on the farm this year, he called me Bob because he got fed up trying to remember Reuben and I've been called Bob ever since.

He wanted to put me in charge of the boys because I had been there a long time and knew my way around. But I refused because I needed a full time job. I had an interview with Hedley Peters, the auctioneer, along with another bloke, and when I came out he asked me how I got on and when I told him he said that he'd told them he got first and second grades and so he got the job. On hearing that I didn't get the job Roy Andrews said to me, 'Go and see my father at half past six tonight.'

He lived in a big house in Park Road, called Roomagh, it's not there now it's a housing estate. His dad told me to go down to Pullen's Garage on Tuesday morning and report to Mr Bushell, that was the day after August Bank Holiday in 1943. It was then that the penny dropped and I realised I was being employed by Pullen's Garage; I thought I was being employed by the farm.

When I was young two of my hobbies were the sea cadets and going to the pictures. When I started work I gave up the sea cadets and joined the Home Guard. The reason for this was because Roy Andrews was a second lieutenant.

I was called up for National Service in 1945 and went in the Royal Navy. When I was demobbed, in 1947, I reported back to Pullen's and stayed there till 1959. I spent very happy years there.

PETER MANTLE

Living on the periphery of the town, in Chalkwell Road, was very peculiar. We were only just in Milton but felt very much a part of it, body and soul. The heart of Milton was politically controlled by the Labour Party. I met Janice, my wife when I was seventeen. She came from the other side of the High Street, which was the dividing line between Sittingbourne and Milton and if you lived on that side you didn't go into Milton.

It was a daunting experience for her when she came to meet my mum and dad in our front room. When we spent our evenings there I had to pay for the coal. There were three children in our family; I was one of twins, the other one died at birth. Janice was always very nervous when she came to our house.

I was an apprentice tool maker at Kent Alloys in Strood, I travelled up by motor bike, then after a while in a car and towards the end by train. So it was always quite late in the evening when I saw Janice. While we were courting she eventually became used to coming into Milton on her own. I don't know why people were reluctant to come into Milton but on one occasion when my vehicle broke down I phoned the AA and at first he didn't want to come. I eventually persuaded him to do so.

Only known surviving (PLP) Public Leaning Post made by Littlewoods Engineering, Milton Hill.

On the banks of the creek, where the barges were moored, were PLPs, public leaning posts, we used them as our wickets and goal posts. Some years later the area was being redeveloped and I spoke to one of the contractors and asked him if I could have one of the posts. He said that I could but I would have to dig it out and cart it away. It was a real one not one of the mock ones. What I didn't realise was that it was under the curb with a large flange attached. It was cast by Littlewoods and Sons the local foundry on Milton Hill. I gave some kids a shilling each to dig it out; it took them all afternoon to do it and they put it into the boot of my car; it stuck out at the back and it was so heavy that it forced the car up at the front and down at the back. Just as I was about to pull away a chap asked me if I was going to put it in my back garden as a souvenir, I told him, yes. It now takes pride of place in my back garden and my son uses it as a wicket.

DON KINGSNORTH

I had to leave school before I finished my education as my father had to retire and I had to help with the household expenses. I started work with an electrician named Collins. He had place in William Street but he was a mean old man and I couldn't stand him for long so I found a job at the Export Packing Company at the top of Wellwinch Road. I was put in the sawmill department and this determined my whole future working life.

When I first started work we did not have television so we spent a lot of evenings up on the Rec; by we I mean myself and the friends I went to school with. We became friendly with the local lassies who we met there. My particular favourite was a girl called Edna Clarke. I was called up to do my National Service in 1950 so just before I left I said goodbye to all my friends saying to them not to expect any letters from me as I wasn't fond of putting pen to paper. On reflection I don't think this went down well with Edna, so that, effectively, was the end of our relationship.

On returning to civilian life in 1952 I resumed my old job at the Export Packing where my sister Betty was also working. She was courting (what a nice word) a fellow called Garrett Stone from Sittingbourne, he was a very laid back gentleman. Meeting him and his friends opened up a new chapter in my life. His nickname was Boney and his friends aspired to names like Sqiffer, Scorch, Bo, Twinners and Bill-Bob, (William Shilling). I remember one summer when there were a lot of road works going on with pipes being laid. Some of the labourers on the hob were Irish lads who stayed at the lodging house known as "The KIP'. They liked a drink after work and most of them used our local, which was the closest, and if you were to look out of the window at about 7.00pm you would see, coming down the Milton Road, a group of them. There was not one small one amongst them. They were all perfect gentlemen and great to talk to. I know the landlord was very sorry to see them go when the work was finished. They were good for business.

Marshal Brunger and his wife Doris were regulars of the White Horse. They lived in Charlotte Street and in his younger days he worked in the brickfields, then later on for the council. He was a real Milton man and he was noted for his ability to catch fish and rabbits. He also knew where the best fruit grew. During the war my father would ask him to come round and skin a few rabbits for our Christmas dinner. This was the only treat available then due to food rationing.

Bob Fynn, a friend of mine, used to make a bit of money by going out and picking horseradish which he put in jars and sold. When I became unemployed for a short while I took him out in my car to see if we could drum up customers from further afield; but we didn't have much luck. Because Milton had streams running through it and there were underground springs at the Meads all sorts of things used to grow wild. I was particularly fond of collecting the watercress which grew there. We often went out to places like Milstead where chestnut trees grew and in the autumn came home with pockets full.

One local character who I mentioned earlier was Freddy Mockett and he was a customer in the pub. Most of what I know about Fred was told to me by my parents, apparently he was a grafter who started his business pushing a barrow round the streets selling fruit and vegetables. He worked very long hours and it wasn't long before he was able to open his shop. Even when he was older he continued to go round selling goods from his lorry on a Sunday and would arrive at the White Horse at about 1.30pm when he would stop for a pint of beer and do his trade at the same time. He became well respected in the town.

Another caller at the pub on a Sunday morning was a man selling shellfish. He did good business and the pub was soon full of people eating cockles, winkles, whelks and such.

8. MEMORIES OF PUB LIFE

ROY JARMAN

My mates and I used to spend the weekends going round the pubs. Come Monday we had no money left so I would borrow some off gran and she would lend it to me on condition that it was paid back on Friday evening. By then I owed her almost all my wage packet so what was left only lasted till Monday.

RON SHEPHERD

We used the pub called the 'Milton Arms' next to the mill gates when we were fourteen; the landlady used to serve us in the back room. The amount of beer we could buy for a £1 was enough for five of us to get drunk on. The cheapest beer you can get now is £2 a pint. The police in those days would tell us off and I had a couple of clips round the ear and that was the end of it. We would have a few drinks on a Saturday night, come along Milton High Street having a good sing song and if we saw a policeman we would stop singing, once we'd gone past him we would start singing again. They never took any notice!

PETER MANTLE

In the early fifties the pubs were flourishing and although

mum and dad went to the pub regularly they each had their favourite one. The one at the bottom of Milton Hill was called the 'King's Arms' and only once have I ever seen another pub like it and that was in the East End of London. The owner was called Alice and she was cross-eyed so you never knew who she was looking at. The pub was always full of service men, soldiers and sailors. You could guarantee that the evening would always end up in a fight. Mum and dad used to go down there on a Saturday night because it was lively and one particular night when I was with them, Alice said, 'Who's going to play the piano?'

This piano was in the back room, which was supposed to be the children's room, and the only other furniture in there was broken chairs. No one volunteered to play so Alice got the job. Everyone was singing and people were serving themselves by leaning over the counter and pushing the pumps. After some time the floor was awash with beer and people were paddling in it.

There was a sailor standing on his head, drinking a pint, when a bloke came in with a monkey. Inevitably it all ended up in a fight. The significant thing is that the man with the monkey lived two doors away up the hill. The monkey had been brought in by a service man some time earlier and he was looking for the bloke who sold it to him because it had got a cold and he didn't know what to do with it. His name was Green and he belonged to a very traditional Milton family. Some drunken soldier advised him to put it in the oven and this caused another fight that spilled out into the road. They called the police but it was left to Alice to sort it out.

Suddenly there came a cry, Here come the gypsies!'

We looked out and saw, in spite of the poor lighting, a horse and cart with the man driving it standing up. It was going so fast that sparks were coming off the horse's hooves and men were lying down on the cart so they didn't fall off. It was like a scene from Ben Hur. The families with children thought it was time they went home and the service men became united and decided to fight the gypsies instead of each other. That was a typical Saturday night at the 'King's Arms'.

From there we went to the 'Green Dragon' round the corner in Flushing Street leaving them fighting. If you could play the piano and sing you could go round the pubs in Milton all weekend without spending any money and having a good drink. One man, Tich May I remember, was a good pianist and he lives in Court Regis. He was disabled but happy go lucky as could be. His party piece was to bang on the piano lid with his knuckles. He would rat-tat-tat and put his hand to his ear and when he was feeling thirsty he'd put words to his rapping and sing 'I'd like another pint.' He would spend an hour in each pub and then move on.

DON KINGSNORTH

Although my mates and I spent some evenings at the Rec after we left school I also became interested in pubs; being a big lad and looking older than I was, I would visit the 'Crown and Anchor' with my father. Tim Blackman was the landlord in those days, a nice old fellow who would always put on his 'cheesecutter' hat when he called time. He must have had a very

The 'Alexandra', Charlotte Street, closed in 1957 demolished more than 10 years later.

bad memory because he would stand at the door and say to everyone as they went out, ' Good night er. um!'

It was worth waiting till last orders just to watch the ritual.

Through the influence of my sister's boy friend, Garrett, most of the mob used to come to Milton to sup the ale and we started to patronise the 'Alexandra'. The landlady was called Nancy Morgan and she married Jack Bunting and we became great friends. The pub became known as the Nuthouse.

Things went on at the pub that were a talking point for years; for example: one old fellow, Long Tom, was a good drinker and although no longer in his prime was goaded into riding a bike down the stairs. This he did with no after effects, whatsoever. One of the locals was Jerry Light, a totter, who worked on his own behind an old brick air raid shelter in Millen Road. He was a retired traveller who was well liked by everyone and always ready for a challenge. One Sunday lunch time session a fellow named Jessie Read was boasting about how much cider he could put away, so Jerry said, 'If you think you can hold your booze I'll give you a shilling for every pint you can drink.'

At that, Jessie's eyes lit up and by closing time he had downed ten pints so he had a good drink and was 10 shillings in pocket. In the fifties this was a nice handy sum. But the punch line was that Jessie headed off to Sittingbourne High Street, made a nuisance of himself and was arrested for being drunk and disorderly. He was fined more than he had made, he wasn't in the least bit upset and it made a good talking point for a long time afterwards.

The 'Alexandra' didn't have a spirit licence so at some point during a good Saturday jug up one of us would suggest going up the 'Foresters' for a couple of tots of 'laughing gas'. Off we would go with any women who were with us and spend an hour playing dice for drinks.

On Boxing Night 1955 things were swinging with music being provided by a customer playing the piano. Towards closing time some joker suggested taking the piano outside and giving everyone a tune. This is just what we did and gradually it was pushed further and further up Charlotte Street, stopping every few yards so the pianist could play a tune and we would all sing. By the time we reached the next pub, half way up the street it was gone closing time. Some miserable person must have reported us because as we were in full voice, around the corner from Watson's Hill came a car full of policemen; this was before the age of the panda car. They were very nice but said we had to stop because Christmas was over and suggested that we take the piano back where it came from. They took a few names to make it look serious.

Another good pianist was Emmie Saunders; her husband, Bill, used to do shift work at Bowater's Mill and when he was on the 2-10 shift he would call in the pub for a pint on his way home. As he came through the door at five past ten his pint was already being pulled and as he handed over a ten shilling note he always said take for two and before the barmaid got back with his change the glass was empty and he was ready for his second. Sometimes Bill and Emmie would entertain us by singing a duet, usually the same song.

The 'Foresters' Charlotte Street, one of six remaining public houses.

It was a very regular thing during the weekend lunch hours for a game of cards to be played in the 'Alexandra'. When Jerry Light or one of the other good drinkers said to Nancy give us a drink that was the signal for a crate of brown ale and one of light to be placed on the bar with the opener and we just helped ourselves.

In 1957 Bowater's wanted to expand and so they bought the land from the bottom of the street up to the 'Foresters' and demolished the row of houses and the 'Alexandra' so we took our custom to the 'Foresters'. Nancy became the landlady of the 'Three Hats' but we didn't fancy going there as it was quieter than we were used to. We only used the 'Foresters' for a short while because we upset the other regulars by being too happy and enjoying ourselves. The pub across the road was called the 'White Horse' so we took our custom there.

Over the years the landlords changed regularly but one couple, Cecil and Emmie, started to let rooms to contractors working in the area. One of the lodgers we got on well with was a Scot called Davy Grey. He liked to have a game of cards and he joined our card school. He also liked to bet on horses and for the three or four years that the contract lasted he came with me and my friends to Ascot; we never won very much but we always enjoyed ourselves.

The regulars of the pub invited half a dozen of us to make up a reserve dart team, more out of politeness than anything; we accepted and surprised the regulars by winning more competitions than they did. Our first full season was great; we won through to the final of the L.V.A knockout and had to play the New Inn in the final. Our skipper was Perce Parkes and his enthusiasm rubbed off on the rest of us. The final was played in a dance hall in Cryalls Lane on the stage used by dance bands. We won 4-0! Perce filled up the cup with whisky and passed it round the team, which comprised Perce, his brother Sam, Squiffer, Scorch, Rush, Boney, Bob Finn and me.

Like the Alexandra, the White Horse didn't have a spirit licence so during the evening we would visit the 'Three Hats' or

'The White Hart' in Milton High Street for a few drops of giggle juice. We would often race there and although I sometimes won I could never see the point of trying to be first because the winner had to get the first round. It was uphill all the way and so the winner was out of breath and couldn't enjoy his drink. Still they were crazy days.

At this time Cecil and Emmie decided to apply for a spirit licence and started a petition for the customers to sign. We had to give our occupation as well as our name and there were slight changes to make it look more upmarket. Lorry drivers mates became transport managers, road sweepers were civil engineers and I, being a wood machinist, became a saw mill foreman overnight. This must have impressed the powers that be as the licence was granted with no trouble at all. In 1966 Cecil and Emmie decided to retire; as they were friends we were sad to see them go.

At the end of 1967 the pub was taken over by Tom and Barbara Cullen who came from Queenborough. When they moved in they brought with them Barb's mother, brothers

Barbara and Tom Cullen behind the bar of the White Horse, mine hosts for 20 years.

Dennis and Jimmy and sister Christine. That wasn't the lot, though. She also had another three sisters and one brother. Tom, who originally hailed from Sittingbourne continued to do shift work at the mill while they established themselves. They were an extremely popular couple and Barbara was noted for her great laugh, which, when in full flow could stop the traffic in Sittingbourne High Street. Tom became a good friend and he would help anyone in need. One thing the regulars could be sure of was plenty of good-humoured jesting and 'mickey taking'. As it was nearly Christmas they asked me if I had done any bar work as they might need help. I had a few practice sessions and it was a good job I did as the place was packed to the doors the whole Christmas. They ran a social club and every year held a dinner and dance at Sittingbourne Town Hall. One year the entertainer was Michael Barrymore, just before he became famous. Many good times we had over the next few years until I moved away.

9. PRESENT AND FUTURE

If Thomas Bradbury, a Miltonian business man from the sixteenth century, were to be transported to Milton Regis today he would know where he was. His house is still there and he could still have a drink in the 'Three Hats'; although it wasn't called that in his day. Even though most of the buildings now have shop fronts the original structures are there in the upper parts. He would, of course, wonder what had happened to the market, with all its familiar sights and sounds.

Stepping outside the High Street the greatest shock for him would be the state of the creek. Once it was one of England's busiest waterways, but it is silted up now and the ebb and flow of the tide does not produce enough water for the red sailed barges. The smell of fish and the shouts of the bargemen as they loaded and unloaded their cargoes have vanished. The town is quieter and definitely a pleasanter place to live with modern sanitation, plumbing and paved streets.

Edward Littlewood, the owner of the engineering works on

Milton Hill, who died in 1935 would also be amazed at the changes in the town if he were alive today. The Holy Trinity Church is still there, but the Congregational and St Paul's Churches have gone as have the workhouse and the Fire Brigade. The latter amalgamated with Sittingbourne in 1938. The light railway, which carried workers and commodities between the mill and Ridham Dock, is a popular tourist attraction and runs between Sittingbourne and Kemsley.

*The wheel of the Periwinkle Mill, in 1999.
It is hoped that this will become a museum*

The pavilion in the Recreation Ground, which he worked so hard to have built was demolished in the 1950s; the ground is surrounded by streets of pleasant houses. In fact, the greatest difference he would find would be in the residential part of the town. The rows of houses that crowded round the head of the creek, such as Flushing Street, Bridge Street and The Wall, are no longer there. Most of this land is now waste ground although there are a few industrial buildings, and some sheltered housing for the elderly has been built. Houses have sprung up in different parts of the town; bright modern homes to replace the ones that suffered floods on a regular basis. The land north of the Holy Trinity Church was used to create an estate in the 1980s, called Church Milton, and this cluster of attractive houses, in effect, joined Milton Regis and Kemsley together.

Milton Creek in 1999 with the tide coming up.

The industries, which dominated the town for many years, are there no longer; only the mills, now owned by UK Paper, are still operating but they employ far fewer people than they used to. Instead, smaller local industries, such as those on the Trinity Trading Estate provide employment, giving local people more choice. The heavy traffic that used to pass through the centre of the town, to the detriment of the old buildings, now uses Mill Way, the road through the trading estate. St Paul's Street has been extended, and the Staplehurst Road Link connects with the A249 and Key Street.

Of the twenty five public houses which served the townsfolk in 1908 only six remain. This shows that not only has the town changed but so have the habits of the residents. The Asda supermarket, which has been built on the old brickfield opposite the trading estate, has brought mixed blessings for the town. It does bring in people from other areas but, of course, it also takes trade away from the local shops.

1932 Talbot owned by Sharon & Phil Richards of Groveshurst, on show at ceremony of refurbishment of Milton Regis High Street.

On June 7th 1973 the local council amalgamated with those of the Isle of Sheppey and Faversham to become part of the group which served as the shadow council before becoming, in April 1974, Swale District Council. As Queenborough was part of the Swale area the council applied to have their borough status conferred on the whole district. This was granted on 20th January 1978 and Swale Borough Council came into being. The people of Milton Regis have to go into Sittingbourne for most things now. The council offices, town hall, police station and library are all in Central Avenue, which was built in the 1960s. The post office is still in Milton High Street and there are shops there that cater for the needs of local residents. Still very much a focal point of the town, as it has been for 550 years, is Court Hall. It is now a museum and is cared for by the Sittingbourne Society and Archaeology Group. At the beginning of 1999 the area surrounding it was refurbished and officially opened by the Mayor of Swale for 1998/9, Councillor Gerry Lewin. The drinking fountain, which for many years stood in the recreation ground has been restored and put back in its original position, next to Court Hall.

1938 Morris 8 P.O. Van, owned by Ken Wilson of Iwade, on show at ceremony of refurbishment of Milton Regis High Street.

The trust that Thomas Bradbury left to the poor in his will is still in operation. Some of this money goes to the infants' school at the Butts. This school is now known as Milton Court County Primary and the junior school in Middletune Avenue is now called Regis Manor Junior School.

As the century draws to a close plans are under way to improve the land at Church Marshes. A pathway down to the creek will allow people access to fishing and walking activities and picnic grounds will be laid out. Plans to make Periwinkle Mill, in Church Street, a museum with a working wheel are already in progress. If these and other ideas come to fruition more people will come into the town and the residents of Milton Regis will be able to look forward to an interesting and prosperous future.

The road names are echoes of the past. Names such as Saffron Way, Dean Road, Periwinkle Close, Kingsmill Close, Middletune Avenue, Cherry Close, Windmill Road and Millen Road are a reminder of a way of life that has gone forever. As long as Court Hall stands the illustrious history of Milton Regis will always be remembered.

The Authors - Beryl Kingsnorth and Dennis J Smith pictured by the newly replaced drinking fountain at the ceremony to open the refurbishment of the Court Hall area in April 1999.

PUBLIC HOUSES IN MILTON REGIS IN 1908

The George Inn	-	High Street
The Malt Shovel	-	High Street
The Sadlers Arms	-	High Street
The Crown and Anchor	-	Bridge Street
The Jolly Sailor	-	Flushing Street
The Prince of Wales	-	The Wall
The Milton Arms	-	The Wall
The Green Dragon	-	King Street
The Good Intent	-	King Street
The Cumberland Arms	-	Mill Street
The Watermans Arms	-	Mill Street
The Ship	-	Milton Hill
The Kings Arms	-	Milton Hill
The Sailors Home	-	Milton Quay
The Lion Inn	-	Church Street
The Alexandra	-	Charlotte Street
The Grapes	-	Chalkwell Road
The Kentish Hotel	-	Hawthorn Road
The Kings Head	-	Chalkwell Road
*The White Hart	-	Milton High Street
*The Three Hats	-	Milton High Street
*The Foresters	-	Charlotte Street
*The White Horse	-	Charlotte Street
*The Prince Alfred	-	Arthur Street
*The Crown Inn	-	Chalkwell Road

Of these Public Houses sixteen were still in existence in the 1950s.

*Only the last six on the list are open in 1999, the Crown is now called the Stumble Inn.

GLOSSARY

Almshouse	Small home built for the poor from charity funds.
Bob	A slang word for a shilling.
Bogie	A small truck used to transport coal, rubble etc.
Chancel	The part of a church near the altar for the clergy and choir. Usually kept separate from the main part of the church by a screen or steps.
Coke	Substance left after gas is extracted from coal used as fuel for boilers and fires.
Gaffer	Term for a foreman.
Gas mantle	Fragile lacy tube attached to a gas jet to produce a light.
Good wife	The female head of a household.
Guinea	One pound and one shilling.
Half a crown	Two shillings and sixpence.
Home Guard	The British citizen army comprising of men over conscription age and those in reserved occupations. Formed in 1940.
Hoy	A small vessel, rigged as a sloop, used for carrying goods and passengers, usually for small distances.
Lighter	A flat bottomed boat used to transfer good from wharf to ship or ship to ship.
National Service	Two years compulsory service in the armed forces for young men aged 18 lasting from the end of the second world war until 1960.
Prefabs	Small prefabricated houses erected after the war to ease the housing shortage mainly due to bomb damage. These were supposed to last for ten years but some were standing much later than this.

Pug	Clay or loam mixed and prepared for making bricks.
Relay	A device to transmit and receive messages and broadcast.
Sacristy	A room in a church for keepimg vestments in.
Shrapnel	Fragments of a bomb or shell after an explosion. Sometimes made to go off shortly before impact. Named after General Shrapnel who invented the shell. He died in 1842.
Tanner 1	Slang name for a sixpenny piece.
Tanner 2	A person who tans leather.
Tannery	A place where leather is tanned.
Tenter	A frame for stretching cloth.
Zeppelin	A German dirigible airship, i.e. able to be steered or directed.

Conversion of Old to New British Currency

Showing equivalents *Note: 1d. = 00.416 of a new penny (p)*

Old (d)	New (p)	Old (d)	New (p)	Old (d)	New (p)	Old (d)	New (p)
1d	00.417p	5/1	25.417p	10/1	50.417p	15/1	75.417p
2	00.833	5/2	25.833	10/2	50.833	15/2	75.833
3	01.250	5/3	26.250	10/3	50.250	15/3	76.250
4	01.667	5/4	26.667	10/4	51.667	15/4	76.667
5	02.083	5/5	27.083	10/5	52.083	15/5	77.083
6	02.500	5/6	27.500	10/6	52.000	15/6	77.500
7	02.917	5/7	27.917	10/7	52.917	15/7	77.917
8	03.333	5/8	28.333	10/8	53.333	15/8	78.333
9	03.750	5/9	28.750	10/9	53.750	15/9	78.750
10	04.167	5/10	29.167	10/10	54.167	15/10	79.167
11	04.583	5/11	29.583	10/11	54.583	15/11	79.583
1/-	05.000	6/-	30.000	11/-	55.000	16/-	80.000
1/1	05.417	6/1	30.417	11/1	55.417	16/1	80.417
1/2	05.833	6/2	30.833	11/2	55.833	16/2	80.833
1/3	06.250	6/3	31.250	11/3	56.250	16/3	81.250
1/4	06.667	6/4	31.667	11/4	56.667	16/4	81.667
1/5	07.083	6/5	32.083	11/5	57.083	16/5	82.083
1/6	07.500	6/6	32.500	11/6	57.500	16/6	82.500
1/7	07.917	6/7	32.917	11/7	57.917	16/7	82.917
1/8	08.333	6/8	33.333	11/8	58.333	16/8	83.333
1/9	08.750	6/9	33.750	11/9	58.750	16/9	83.750
1/10	09.167	6/10	34.167	11/10	59.167	16/10	84.167
1/11	09.583	6/11	34.583	11/11	59.583	16/11	84.583
2/-	10.000	7/-	35.000	12/-	60.000	17/-	85.000
2/1	10.417	7/1	35.417	12/1	60.417	17/1	85.417
2/2	10.833	7/2	35.833	12/2	60 833	17/2	85.833
2/3	11.250	7/3	36.250	12/3	61.250	17/3	86.250
2/4	11.667	7/4	36.667	12/4	61.667	17/4	86.667
2/5	12.083	7/5	37.083	12/5	62.083	17/5	87.083
2/6	12.500	7/6	37.500	12/6	62.500	17/6	87.500
2/7	12.917	7/7	37.917	12/7	62.917	17/7	87.917
2/8	13.333	7/8	38.333	12/8	63.333	17/8	88.333
2/9	13.750	7/9	38.750	12/9	63.750	17/9	88.750
2/10	14.167	7/10	39.167	12/10	64.167	17/10	89.167
2/11	14.583	7/11	39.583	12/11	64.583	17/11	89.583
3/-	15.000	8/-	40.000	13/-	65.000	18/-	90.000
3/1	15.417	8/1	40.417	13/1	65.417	18/1	90.417
3/2	15.833	8/2	40.833	13/2	65.833	18/2	90.833
3/3	16.250	8/3	41.250	13/3	66.250	18/3	91.250
3/4	16.667	8/4	41.667	13/4	66.667	18/4	91.667
3/5	17.083	8/5	42.083	13/5	67.083	18/5	92.083
3/6	17.500	8/6	42.500	13/6	67.500	18/6	92.500
3/7	17.917	8/7	42.917	13/7	61.917	18/7	92.917
3/8	18.333	8/8	43.333	13/8	68.333	18/8	93.333
3/9	18.750	8/9	43.750	13/9	68.750	18/9	93.750
3/10	19.167	8/10	44.167	13/10	69.167	18/10	94.167
3/11	19.583	8/11	44.583	13/11	69.583	18/11	94.583
4/-	20.000	9/-	45.000	14/-	70.000	19/-	95.000
4/1	20.417	9/1	45.417	14/1	70.417	19/1	95.417
4/2	20.833	9/2	45.833	14/2	70.833	19/2	95.833
4/3	21.250	9/3	46.250	14/3	71.250	19/3	96.250
4/4	21.667	9/4	46.667	14/4	71.667	19/4	96.667
4/5	22.083	9/5	47.083	14/5	72.083	19/5	97.083
4/6	22.500	9/6	47.500	14/6	72.500	19/6	97.500
4/7	22.917	9/7	47.917	14/7	72.917	19/7	97.911
4/8	23.333	9/8	48.333	14/8	73.333	19/8	98.333
4/9	23.750	9/9	48.750	14/9	73.750	19/9	98.750
4/10	24.167	9/10	49.167	14/10	74.167	19/10	99.167
4/11	24.583	9/11	49.583	14/11	74.583	19/11	99.583
5/-	25.000	10/-	50.000	15/-	75.000	20/-	£1-00